Managing Media Creating Character

Using the Technology Kids Crave to Develop the Character God Desires

Be Brave! Kelly Newcom

Kelly Newcom

Founder of Brave Parenting

BRAVE
parenting

To Angela,

The bravest friend and parent I've ever known. You are the reason I began writing. It was always your dream to write a book, but heaven called you home. Your life continued to inspire me through every step of this book writing journey. As you predicted, it has been a wild ride.

CONTENTS

Acknowledgements   i

Preface: Wherever this book finds you   1

Introduction: Why character matters more than media   7

1   Patience: Wait for the privilege   20

2   Respect: Boundaries for everyone   42

3   Kindness: Read what they type, coach what they say   64

4   Honesty: No lies, nothing deleted   88

5   Self-Control: Limited time and quantity   107

6   Humility and Modesty: No selfies, no MMS   129

7   Self-Worth: Delayed access to social media   153

8   Maintaining Sanity   176

Epilogue   194

About the Author   203

About Brave Parenting   205

Defining Each Generation   206

Common Texting Acronyms   207

Notes   208

ACKNOWLEDGMENTS

I am abundantly grateful for Jesus Christ, my Savior and King. He deserves any and all glory for this book, not I.

To my husband and best friend, Ryan. Thank you for believing in me, giving me time to write, correcting my mixed metaphors, being an amazing father, and packing the kids' lunches every single day. You are the very best part of life. To my seven children, who challenge and transform me in the best ways possible. I love you and every crazy moment God has blessed us with. Thank you for supporting me (even if you don't always agree with my message.)

To my circle: Chelsea, Shelley, Ashley, and Debbie. These words would never have been penned if not for Colorado, your discernment, anointing, and prayers. You continually help me maintain sanity in life, for which I'm tremendously thankful.

To Maria, Tracy and my pharmacy staff who supported me unwaveringly every day as I dreamed, discussed, and lamented over this book. Thank you for your sacrifices in accommodating my writing, speaking, and raising seven kids.

Thank you also to my Brave Parenting community, knowing there is a remnant of Christians who deeply desire to raise image bearers of Jesus inspires me to be even more brave and speak out.

Wherever This Book Finds You

I've been there.

Whatever made you pick up this book: concern over your child's online activity, despair from feeling out of control with devices, lack of tech knowledge, lack of cultural media standards, anger over what your child has done, regret for what you've already allowed, fear for your child's future relationships, humility knowing you've not set a good example, or you are feeling like a lost sheep without a shepherd — all of it, I've been there and felt it all along with you.

I am a mom of seven foster-adopted children. If you multiply my number of children by each child's friends and peer influences, you can imagine the amount of phone, device, and internet related drama I've either dealt with or heard about.

What makes my situation unique, besides having seven children who look nothing like me, is how I approach all things relating to technology with my children. First, you should know that my children came to me at varying ages: a ten-month-old and five-year-old in 2007, a fifteen-year-old in 2013, and her four siblings ages seven, eight, ten and eleven in 2014. With them, many sinful inclinations and worldly tendencies were brought into my home. What my children witnessed and experienced in broken biological homes and foster care made me the fiercely vigilant parent I am. I could never make the assumption, "My child will never do that," or worse, "My child has nothing to hide from me." Knowing they had spent a combined total of thirty-one years in the foster care system, my stance has always been, "Yep, there is a good chance my kid would do that."

I desire nothing more in life than to see my children restored and redeemed. I want to take the ashes of their trauma and create souls of beautiful character ready to face the world without the chains of their past. But technology and media have been stumbling blocks — or even cinder blocks — weighing my children down and preventing their character growth. They crave the escape of video games, the excitement of horror movies, and the semblance of importance and fame on social media.

As I sought the Lord every day for insight and understanding, I realized I was not enough to fix all of this, but Jesus was. The Holy Spirit gave me wisdom to handle every situation and led me on a journey of creating character through the one thing that dominates their lives: technology.

This book details how the Lord enabled me to manage the screens and media for my seven children while at the same time reinforce the importance of character. My story is not perfect or finished. I have my share of media horror stories, but I also have tales of successful character building. This is my hope for you. Each chapter provides a God-honoring character strength along with a boundary or media standard to help build that character. Additionally, you'll find further evidence, conviction, and purpose as to why you must try to manage media, along with practical methods to actually do the work. I will warn you though; I don't call it Brave Parenting for nothing.

In order to manage media and create character you must be brave. You will be battling against some of the wealthiest, most intelligent, and most influential minds in the world today who are trying to program your child's brain otherwise. Apple, Google, Facebook, and Amazon have such massive influence today that we cannot attempt to contend with them without Jesus. Luckily for us, Jesus is still more powerful than any Google search algorithm.

> APPLE, GOOGLE, FACEBOOK, AND AMAZON HAVE SUCH MASSIVE INFLUENCE TODAY THAT WE CANNOT ATTEMPT TO CONTEND WITH THEM WITHOUT JESUS.

Since the day I became a mother of seven children, I have been beyond overwhelmed with the task of parenting. Regardless how many children you have, chances are you feel overwhelmed too. I persevere doing the only thing I know: hold on to God's promise to, "Be strong and brave. Get to work. Don't be afraid. Don't lose hope...." (1 Chr 28:20 NIRV)

These words came from King David to his son Solomon, whose task was to build the temple to honor God. Fellow brave parent, you and I have been given the task to build up children of character to honor God. It takes strength, bravery, and hard work to raise children in our current times. Most days you, like me, probably feel far from strong or brave. Allow the Holy Spirit to use that verse as a constant reminder to not be afraid or lose hope, but only to be strong and brave. Our children's character will be built and they will honor God, but first we must get to work.

Are you ready? Whether or not you feel strong and exude bravery, you can do the work. Wherever you are, whatever you feel, whatever you've already experienced — you have the ability and opportunity to change the world, one child at a time.

Now if this book finds you with faith other than Christianity or without faith at all, you will still find welcome, help, and hope within these pages. While the book developed out of my personal prayers for my children, study of God's written word, and inspiration from the Holy Spirit, I know it can be applied in any home and lead to triumphant gains in character. Because, in the end, we all want kids of great character. So whether you know Jesus or not, the value of these pages still holds true, and I am praying you meet Him through these pages.

Wherever this finds you as a parent, Managing Media Creating Character offers something for everyone:

If you have BABIES . . . read this book and act. Your child watches your passive and active media consumption from the moment he can see. How you manage your media and the media your baby consumes will affect his brain development and character. What feels so easy and harmless may be doing permanent damage. Decide now how you will handle media throughout your child's life. Don't focus on making them tech savvy; the very nature of the world today will teach them. Instead, focus on building problem solving skills, teaching them to make good choices and building resilience. These are the things not taught by screens. Then, pass this book on to someone you know who has older kids. Encourage them to be proactive. Their kids may be your next babysitter (and influencer).

If you have TODDLERS . . . read closely and hang on every word. You may be blinded by your toddler's cuteness and how well behaved she is when playing on an iPad, but she will soon be in elementary school where kindergarten phone ownership will be the new norm. Tablets are not pacifiers and their use must be monitored. If you haven't made firm decisions as to how much screen-time is allowed and what types of media can be consumed, do this now. Most importantly, be ever cognizant of your media habits in front of your child. Your time for change and self-reflection is right now, if not yesterday, because they will grow to mimic everything they've seen.

If you have ELEMENTARY-AGE children . . . read and re-read, then share with all your kids' friends' parents and encourage them to read this book. This is the tender age where it all begins, when the standards and boundaries for phones and devices are pushed and muddled. This is when the fun can turn into pain, and connection becomes competition. Kids at this age are learning technology at school — taught by teachers and shared by students. You have to stay ahead both in knowledge and in modeling. Bravery begins here. Starting off on the right foot and setting clear, unwavering standards during the elementary years will revolutionize your middle school and high school experiences.

If you have MIDDLE SCHOOL-AGE children . . . read and reassure yourself it is not too late to invoke standards while teaching character. Unfortunately, you are in the war zone right now. Peer and cultural pressure, in addition to experimentation, are at their peak. Kids this age are easily influenced and swayed, so it's crucial that you continue to be their primary influencer! Therefore, your media consumption behaviors matter more than ever. Do not give up! Your children desperately need you to care about them, even though they will not show it. Despite what you think, they want you to keep them safe. They are on a roller coaster of the highs, lows, twists, and turns of identity and peer pressure. You must be the lap bar that keeps them secure. You and your child can absolutely win this war. It's yours to fight.

If you have HIGH SCHOOLERS . . . don't accept that unlimited internet, smartphones, and social media are a teenager's right — and do nothing. Read to educate yourself about what she is doing on her phone or what he is doing on the internet. If they live in your home or you pay for the phone, the door is still open to share your wisdom. Appropriate media use and phone communication behavior are much needed for the years ahead. Colleges and employers are watching. If you have younger children as well, they too are watching and learning. Model the behavior you want to see, talk about it, plant seeds, and build character. They are listening.

If you are a GRANDPARENT . . . your media usage or technological ignorance can have just as much influence over your grandchildren as their peers. Read this book to understand the struggles faced by parents and children today. Allowing your grandchild to play on your phone isn't necessarily a harmless activity anymore. If your phone, devices, computers, etc. aren't locked down, you could be providing open access for your grandchild's dangerous activity. If you have an active or semi-active role in raising your grandchild, read this book with Mom or Dad to be on the same page where media allowances and usage are concerned. A united front is harder to break through.

Why Character Matters More Than Media

It was a seemingly normal Wednesday evening in May, 2015. The almost-summer sun hung in the sky just long enough to make the 8 pm bedtime painful for my elementary-age children. We were only ten days away from the end of another school year and our growing anticipation for unstructured days rivaled our apathy toward the remaining days of schoolwork.

Around 9:30 pm, my husband returned home from picking up my oldest daughter from the high school. She was seventeen years old, finishing her junior year, but had yet to obtain her driver's license. So when she wanted to attend school events, such as the powder-puff football game that evening, we were her chauffeur.

My daughter and I stood in the office just off of our kitchen as I listened to her recant the evening events with the familiar, dramatic flair that occurs after she has had a fun time. Suddenly, while she spoke, flashing lights went off inside her shirt. My eyes showed confusion and concern as she tried to cover it up and keep my attention on her story.

I wasn't fooled. "Why is your shirt lighting up?"

"What? It's not! You're crazy," she said with a nervous laugh.

My husband, Ryan, stood making coffee just inside the kitchen. Yes, we drink coffee at 9:30 pm. He overheard me and quickly joined our conversation. He skipped all further questions. "Hand over the phone inside your shirt, right now."

She rebuked him, explaining how her phone was right there in her hand.

As Ryan and I stood in front of her, angry, unwavering, and impassable, shame and cortisol took over her brain. "You're crazy! I freaking hate it here! I don't have anything in my shirt! "

I knew whatever was on this 'burner' phone must be extremely incriminating.

"If I want to throw my life away, it's my life, so just let me. I will leave here the first chance I get, so I don't have to live under your stupid rules!"

An hour of discussion later, she threw the phone at us and walked out the front door. "Did she just leave?" We stared at each other in disbelief.

We walked outside, she was nowhere to be found. Hours later, nowhere to be found.

The next day, I contacted the school counselor, confirming she was both in attendance and safe. Despite the counselor's attempt to talk her into coming home, she wasn't budging. During the days of her absence in our home, my husband and I dug into her phone and the home computer she used the most. We searched for clues that would indicate where she might be staying, and we explored the history of sites she had visited. With her history of social media abuse, dangerous relationships, and sexting all compounded by her childhood trauma, we knew this could have a bad ending.

A few days later, one of her friends from high school arrived on our front porch around 10 pm. I'd met her a few times before. She was two years younger than our daughter, kind and respectful, but I knew she suffered from bullying and peer drama. We invited the girl and her mother, who came as her support, into our home. The mom apologized for their late-night visit.

Through anxious tears the young girl finally stammered, "I know where your daughter is, and you need to go get her. Right now. She told me a man from Michigan is coming to pick her up in the morning, and they are running off together."

Our worst fear of trafficking was confirmed. Ryan grabbed his car keys and hastily asked one more question before bolting out the door, "Where is she?"

After pulling her unwillingly away from a trailer home known to harbor runaway girls, we proceeded into a multi-hour intervention and come-to-Jesus meeting. She finally agreed to come home.

Several weeks later in June, our daughter was acclimating back into family life and doing better. We all attempted to put that particular week behind us, as we learned from our mistakes. School was now out, and summer activities had begun, leaving behind the familiar structure and routine my husband and I rely on for sanity. I was relieved to have survived another school year with seven children and allowed myself to revel in the freedom of summer, forgoing all my typical routine tasks.

The first Sunday after school let out, I felt God beckoning me back to reality. I had an unrelenting and foreboding feeling concerning another daughter. Initially, I assumed it was due to the incessant whispering I heard among my three oldest, my seventeen year old retelling her latest drama. Without fully processing my intuition or planning how to approach it, I felt the Holy Spirit tell me to act immediately. I walked into this daughter's room, found it a disaster, and requested that her phone be handed over until she cleaned her room.

Her eyes grew wide with panic. Tears threatened to fall, revealing emotions rarely seen with her. She begged me not to take the phone. Her reaction confirmed my fears: something was on this phone she was scared to let me see.

At thirteen, she had just finished seventh grade. She'd had her own phone for the past year. We had determined she 'needed' it while she babysat and at away games for sports. We monitored her text messages closely and restricted all access to the Internet and social media. But….in the bustle and drama of the past two weeks, I hadn't checked her phone.

I stole away for a few minutes before church to glimpse at whom she had been texting. I sank into the chair to ward off the feeling of fainting that threatened. A boy, just one year older, whose parents we knew, had been texting her. Their conversation began just two days prior, and in the brief forty-eight hours that had passed, it had escalated from I think you're hot all the way to Let's sneak away so you can give a me a blow job.

It's a good thing I was headed to church after this heart-breaking revelation. I needed Jesus more than ever.

Another month had passed and the Texas summer heat made it hard to be outside unless in a swimming pool. One Sunday afternoon, our family was hanging out with our church life group. I had left early to get ready for my work shift at the pharmacy that evening, leaving Ryan with all of the children. One of our younger boys was bored and interrupted an adult conversation to repeatedly ask if he could play on his iPod, which was at home. "We're going to leave real soon," Ryan told him.

"But I want to play right now!" he began his tantrum.

Mildly frustrated, Ryan jokingly said, "Fine, go get your iPod and play on it." Ryan knew the iPod was at home and assumed our son reconciled this logic as he turned and walked outside.

Fifteen minutes later, Ryan gathered everyone up to head home and this son was nowhere to be found. One of the other children reportedly saw him start running down the street. Remembering their conversation, Ryan quickly deduced our son must have taken him seriously and started walking home to get his iPod. "For crying out loud — you've got to be kidding me!" He hastened everyone into the car and with the windows rolled down, they drove through the neighborhood calling out his name. He was nowhere to be found.

Eventually, Ryan headed out to the highway, the route we take home by car. Two miles from the house our life group was at, they spotted him running alongside the access road of Interstate 10 in the sweltering afternoon heat.

Ryan brought the minivan to a screeching halt beside our son as he ran. "What are you doing!? Get into the car! You scared us half to death!"

Our son, only eight years old, innocently said, "What? I wanted to play my iPod so I was going home to get it."

Oh, the power of the screen. Strong enough to convince a seventeen-year-old to run away, a fourteen-year-old to request oral sex, and an eight-year-old to run alongside a busy highway.

As the rest of summer passed, I was still despaired by the amount of drama these smartphones and devices brought on our family. I began bravely asking other parents basic questions about their kids' screen use.

- Do your children have time limits when they play?
- Do they have open access to the internet? YouTube?
- Do you read their text messages?
- Do they have social media accounts?
- Are they allowed to have their phones in their room at night?
- Can they send and receive pictures?

I received varied answers, but the overwhelmingly, most common response was, "Yeah, I should probably check. I don't really know what they have."

Parents don't know? They aren't checking their kids' phones? Why on earth not? Full access to the internet? Any app they want? There is crazy stuff going on with these phones, and parents have no clue!

My heart broke in despair for a generation of children lost on the internet, and I prayed and begged the Lord for answers. I felt like we had good healthy boundaries for our kids' screen use yet, the power of the screen made them crazy. As I looked around, every kid seemed to be obsessed with their tablet or smartphone. My boundaries and standards meant nothing, if their friends and peers had none. If everyone appears to be face-down and super-connected, my children will want to be as well. But where I saw this obsession and ultra-connectedness, I saw a loss of character. Even more, my mom-heart feared for my future sons and daughters-in-law. Will there be young men and women of character and integrity for my children to marry? Someone needed to start talking about this. This is how Brave Parenting was born.

OWNING OUR PART

I talk to my kids frequently about "owning up" to their part, whether in a sibling dispute or lost homework. I instruct them to "take ownership" for the choices they make that lead to bigger problems. Surely, you do the same. It's a huge part of kids' growth toward competency.

At the risk of sounding like your mother on these pages, I must tell you that it's time for parents to own their part. This means you, me, and every other parent with kids in the home!

Let's evaluate both our personal and parenting choices that have already impacted and continue to influence our children's character development. What part are we responsible for? What do we need to own up to?

First, let us recognize that Generation X (born roughly 1961–81) and early Millennial (about 1981–1995) parents can find an abundance of unfavorable aspects of iGen's (around 1996–present) device and phone obsession. Our society categorizes them as entitled, obsessed, narcissistic, and poor communicators. Woe to us, if we blame iGen for where they are before we, as adults, own our part in allowing it to progress to such a level.

As humans, we are massively reliant on our computers, phones, and the Internet. Digital distraction has become so commonplace, we now consider it normal. Look around at people in restaurants or drivers stopped at traffic lights. Adults are just as tethered to their devices as any child or teen. However, there is one key difference between adults and children. Adults have fully developed frontal lobes of their brains. This is the brain's "control center" for personality, judgment, decision-making, and problem-solving.[1] Frontal lobe development continues throughout adolescence and is complete in a person's early twenties.[2] This, in part, provides scientific reason why the teenage years are so difficult. Their brain just isn't there yet.

Adult brains are there. We are capable of sound judgment, making wise decisions, exerting self-control, communicating effectively, and upholding a moral standard. Adults, in general, are mindful of their digital distraction and dependence and can exert self-discipline to reign it in when needed. The question is, have we?

Despite knowing a world without smartphones, internet, and social media, have parents allowed themselves to be taken over by it all? Do we now believe, as our children do, that the smartphone is the only way to live?

Most of our children do not know or remember a world without texting, video chat, social media, games, apps and Internet. What they do remember is us — adults — glued to our smartphones as they grew up.

Our children watch us. They see our habits, dependencies, and our priorities. They see us on the phone, texting while they tell us a story, editing pictures to make life look rosier, and comparing our lives to those of others on social media, among other things. Fully mature adults, with the ability to discipline themselves and make sound judgments, are completely captivated and controlled by their phones.

Day after day, our kids observe adults who are addicted to devices.

Yet somehow we are frustrated with our young generation for behaving similarly (or worse) due to their immaturity and underdeveloped brains. Our children are mimicking the behaviors we have modeled for them.

DAY AFTER DAY
OUR KIDS
OBSERVE ADULTS
WHO ARE
ADDICTED
TO DEVICES.

We must correct our divergent path. We cannot maintain a "Do as I say, not as I do" mentality, or, sometimes even worse, the "Do as I do" strategy. The path where we assume "If smartphones are good for us, they are equally good for children" is a treacherous one that dead ends in destruction.

Therefore, when we talk about setting a new standard for smartphone usage and paving a new road toward character development, it is essential that we include ourselves, our friends, family, neighbors, schools, sports moms, bible-study groups, etc. Honest and humble discussions must occur within our circles about how our personal smartphone use is affecting our lives, relationships, family, and especially our children.

As we humbly reflect on our role in perpetuating device and smartphone reliance, we should also recognize one of our children's greatest opposing influences: cultural pressure. It used to be that peer pressure influenced and shaped our children, sometimes to a greater degree than parents did. Now, however, it is no longer our children's peers pressuring them. A peer's impact competes on a global scale as culture and media influences become instantly and readily available. With the introduction of smartphones, the Internet became part of our daily wardrobe. Along with it came the major influences of: addiction, bullying, shaming, sexting, pornography, social media comparison and competition, global gossip, FOMO (fear of missing out), and defamation of character.

In order to make any difference in this world and for the kingdom of God, we must recognize and resist this cultural influence and its side-kicks. This may mean we resist the constant influx of news, the perpetual degradation of moral character in movies and television, the conformity to self-promoting habits seen on social media, and the persuasive pull toward pornography and sexualization. Not just in our children's lives, but in ours as well.

When we own our part to model healthy media habits while we resist conforming to cultural media pressures, a beautiful byproduct is created: character.

CHARACTER

Essena O'Neill had an amazing reputation. The Australian Instagrammer was thin, gorgeous, and wealthy for an eighteen-year-old — thanks to her sponsor paid posts. She had over a half-million followers on the social media site where she continually posted jaw-dropping pictures of herself and the vegan food she promoted. In 2015, however, she couldn't stand who she had become and announced her shocking departure from social media claiming her Instagram life was "contrived perfection made to get attention."[3] In a lengthy email newsletter she wrote, "Online it looked like I had the perfect life...yet I was so completely lonely and miserable inside."[4] Essena had lost who she was.

Character is everything. It has been said that character is how God sees us and is who we truly are. Reputation, on the other hand, is how the world sees us. While a good reputation can be a positive reflection of who we are, it can also be contrived. Our target is genuine character — the character God desires.

We are the first generation of parents trying to navigate through this phone/Internet/social media world. Thus far, there has yet to be a standard set. You could say it's been a free-for-all for parents: Tablet for toddler or for kindergartner? Smartphone in second grade or seventh? Allow the Internet or restrict it? Social media in middle school or in high school? Monitor their activity or trust them? Time restrictions or unlimited use?

We aren't the only ones scrambling for a standard with fickle results. School districts everywhere have been forced to choose how technologically savvy their classrooms will be. Some districts have resisted device and smartphone use in the classroom completely, while others have opted to go all in with take-home laptops for every student. Both decisions have been met with controversy and skepticism, leaving only time to reveal which is actually better for the students. Businesses of all types are also attempting to create new policies and standards regarding employee phone and social media use on the clock in an effort to increase productivity and protect company information. Additionally, the government and courts work to interpret current laws in light of new digital and electronic crimes. Are nude pictures texted between teens considered distribution of child pornography? Are cyberbullies liable for the emotional distress or even suicide of their victims?

Since constant media and technology reliance is the new normal for our society, we must use this centerpiece of our lives to teach and develop strong and positive character traits.

This parenting with technology road is unpaved and uncharted. It will not allow us to stroll down its tough terrain at a leisurely pace. We must run to stay ahead of the advancing technology biting at our heels. As we run, leading the way with our own behavior, we can carve a new path under our feet — a new standard for others to follow.

We must mobilize a generation of parents to join us in moving toward this new standard focused on character. Together, with mutual affirmation and mission-minded cohesiveness, we can raise a generation of kids who are better for the technology they possess instead of damaged by its destructive nature.

Despite the ideas pop culture flaunts, it is still the parents' responsibility to teach children the core characteristics that God desires — not YouTube, Google, or the Disney Channel.

Our Creator, who formed us (Ps 139:13) and knows us intimately (Ps 139:1-4), designed us to produce this fruitful character (Gal 5:19-24). Patience, honesty, respect, kindness, modesty, humility, self-control, and self-worth is what the Lord desires to see.

THE CHARACTER YOUR CHILD POSSESSES MUST BE MORE IMPORTANT THAN THE PLEASURE THEY PRESENTLY SEEK.

These characteristics need to be developed in our children . . . and perhaps reestablished in ourselves. Armed with this character, our children will not be less smart or under-experienced in our technology-driven society. Instead, they will be poised to make a positive difference in our world. They will not be lovers of themselves, boastful and proud, disobedient to authority, and ever ungrateful (2 Tim 3:2-5) in a land of entitlement. No, our children will have the character God desires: loving and kind to all (1 Pet 3:8), loyal and obedient to authorities (1 Pet 2:13-17), prioritizing others' needs as greater than their own (Phil 2:3-4), while keeping themselves from being polluted by the world (Jas 1:27).

Valuing character above media/technology is the first step. The character your child possesses must be more important than the pleasure they presently seek. This conviction is crucial, as it will not be easy or comfortable to instill these traits in our oversaturated media world.

The easy path, allowing media/technology without any standards, does not produce proven character. Our kids are not challenged to excellence with a smartphone's utility, nor are they motivated to work hard with its capabilities. Rather, it is through relationships and hard work, discipline and perseverance that ultimately produces character and hope for our future generations.

Let's unite as parents who highly value character to ignite hope for a generation. Together, we can activate a new standard for the glory of God.

> *We also rejoice in our afflictions, because we know that affliction produces endurance, endurance produces proven character, and proven character produces hope.*

> Romans 5:3-4 (CSB)

CHAPTER ONE

Patience:
Wait for the privilege

Good character is not formed in a week or a month. It is created little by little, day by day. Protracted and patient effort is needed to develop good character.[5]

Heraclitus

When the iPhone was introduced in 2007, swarms of eager people hastened to get their hands on one. I was not one of them. I stood back skeptically and waited for everyone else to spend their money and evaluate its true usefulness. It looked cool and all, but was it really worth the money just to have a touch screen?

However, by January 2009 the iPhone culture had permeated my resolve, and I found myself caving in to the overwhelming desire to have an iPhone. Well, it was partly my desire and partly because my mother-in-law wanted to bless me with a late Christmas—early Valentine's Day present. Whoever gave mothers-in-law a bad rap has never met mine. When she asked me what I would like, I eyed my husband, Ryan, to see if the iPhone was an approved device to bring into our Windows PC-only home. He gave his blessing, and I became the proud owner of an iPhone 2. I was in love.

At the time, I had two foster-adopted children, ages eight and three. When we brought them into our home, they lived a fairly simple life of school, church, and home. They watched very little television, only G or PG-rated movies, and occasionally played some Wii Sports. My eight-year-old daughter had no clue what an iPhone was or just how influential it would become in her life. This innocence was completely lost with the thrill and wonder of my new iPhone. As a family, we gathered around and took turns using simple apps like Zippo, Shotgun, and Smule (the app where you blow into the phone like a musical instrument).

Within six months, Ryan jumped onto the iPhone train. Even as we toted our iPhones wherever we went, we never felt burdened from over-connection. We rarely played games on our phones; thus, our children rarely ever asked for our phones to pass the time. My husband and I also resisted the advancement of social media because our only experience with Facebook had been years before through my alumni work with my college sorority. I watched amazing and talented young women fall prey to posting anything and everything without understanding its public nature. Their inappropriate pictures, competition for likes, drama over who posted what and who tagged who, and the ability to "unfriend" all left a sour taste in my mouth for social media. So essentially, our iPhones were just fancy phones for us to communicate with one another.

Something shifted in 2011, both in our society and in my then ten-year-old daughter. Apple, still holding dominance in the market over Google's newly released Android devices,[6] was gearing up to introduce their iPhone 4. The iPad, released just one year earlier, was ready to unveil its redefined iPad 2. At this time, 35 percent of

American adults were using smartphones.[7] As an increasing number of adults rushed to upgrade to the newest version of Apple products, an increasing number of older version iPhones became available. These served as hand-me-down iPhones for the teenagers who sought to have equal phone and Internet freedom. By 2012, 23 percent of teenagers were smartphone users.[8] The mobile migration that had been shifting our communication landscape over the previous ten years from landline to cell phone was now charging full speed ahead toward the beautifully seductive field of smartphones.

Even at the age of ten, my daughter felt the shift. The societal stampede toward smartphones in order to have a "better/easier/cooler life" was both seen and heard with ten-year-old understanding. She reckoned, "If everyone is getting one, well then I, too, need one."

After all, Grandma and Grandpa had just traded their flip phones for their first iPhones, and in her third-grade class, several children were already proudly carrying their own iPhones as well. All of this equated, in her mind, to one fact: she deserved an iPhone.

Despite my cognizance of her attraction toward the phone, I never once considered allowing her to have her own. Apparently, however, she had not only considered this possibility, she dreamed of it. This all hit its apex when Ryan's phone overheated and he needed a replacement. He arrived home from AT&T with my daughter in tow. As I walked outside to meet Ryan upon his return, I was met with one of the sourest looking ten-year-olds I'd ever seen.

With arms crossed hard against her chest, she glared at me. "It's not fair!" she barked.

As I wrestled with my confusion about what could be fair or not fair, Ryan extended his hand brandishing a shiny new iPhone 4, all set up and tucked neatly into a white Otterbox. He proudly exclaimed,

"Your new iPhone." In his kindness, my husband gave the new upgraded phone to me and took over my older phone for himself.

My precious daughter had recalled her dreamy fantasy in which she was handed the iPhone 4 and subsequently became the coolest ten-year-old around. As reality presented a far different scenario, her resentment grew and caused angry tears and words to spill from her.

"Why do you get a new phone? It's not fair to me or Dad!"

I wish I could tell you that I responded with patience and kindness, empathy and understanding. But I did not. My own frustration over her audacious claim telling me what was "fair for me to have" boiled over, leaving both of us standing in a pool of emotion. It's possible I stated something like, "How about you go get a job, work forty hours a week, and buy your own iPhone?" (*Humorously, my daughter did do exactly that during the summer I finished this book. She got a job, saved all her money, and purchased an iPhone 7 plus — a phone we were not willing to buy for ourselves, much less for her.*) Or perhaps I said something even less kind, "On what planet does a parent give a ten-year-old a several-hundred-dollar phone to use when they can't even brush their teeth without being told?" *As it turns out, that planet has recently been identified as Earth.*

This interaction burned into my memory. I hadn't raised a ten-year-old before, so maybe I was naïve, but I was shocked at how quickly she felt entitled to a phone. I would replay this scene hundreds of times in my head and contemplate ways to combat both the entitlement mentality and the impatience she exhibited.

Looking back, I know this was the day God planted a seed of discontent over smartphones within me. Something about it all just wasn't quite right.

I repeatedly asked the Lord over the years, "What is it about these phones and devices that seem to take over people's brains and relationships? Why is the average age to receive a phone decreasing while the number of children exposed to porn and child trafficking simultaneously increases? Am I the only one who sees how bad these phones are for kids?"

God did not drop the answers on me from heaven, but He provided me with lots of hands-on experience as we adopted five more children. Over the course of ten months, I gained a teenager with a phone and four children, ages seven to eleven, who had spent a significant portion of their lives watching television and playing video games.

Aside from what my newly adopted children had been exposed to, the thing that shocked me the most was how patience was not on their radar — not with other people or with technology.

Culture taught them everything is instant. From touch screen devices, to fast food restaurants, to amazon.com, they subconsciously learned that they didn't have to wait long for anything. Impatience, it seemed, was the air they breathed.

With two adults raising seven children, I needed my household to exude patience. Our sanity relied on all of us having patience. Impatience on anyone's part led to chaos. I persistently mulled over and prayed for wisdom, asking, "How do I teach patience to children in an impatient and everything-instant world?" Finally, the fog cleared, and I knew.

Through the technology they love.

The same technological attraction that innately makes them impatient can be used to teach them patience.

PACIFIERS

Consider the parents and children you see in public places. At a restaurant, a tribe of teens sits at a table together, yet they are too entranced with their own phones to eat or talk to one another. At a high school football game, young, adolescent boys play Madden Mobile on their phones in lieu of enjoying the live game unfolding before them. In the department store, a mom scans racks of clothing while her young toddler's drool drips onto her phone while he watches Disney Jr videos. As young as six to nine months old, a child begins to learn that when he whines, cries, demonstrates discomfort, pain, boredom, or a host of annoying behaviors, a screen will be put into his little hands. Entrancing colors and images of Trancit Lite, Baby Piano, Baby Rattle, and Animal Sounds for Baby are available to enable the parents to have peace and quiet on the "one device that never fails to entertain," according to Parents Magazine.[9]

Babies and toddlers learn from the first touch of a screen the joy of immediate response. No other toy, and especially no other human, responds as quickly and consistently as a touch screen device. The effort to reward ratio is dismally low. Persistent dopamine surges rewire the brain similar to the use of cocaine.[10] Sadly, while their age is still counted by months instead of years, young children assimilate the message that screens bring pleasure. And not just pleasure — immediate pleasure.

As a result, the screen becomes the child's soother instead of the parent. The device becomes what comforts an ailing child and relieves boredom instead of the child developing curiosity and discovery. They learn and adapt to all of this almost immediately and unnoticed.

Kids are no longer required to learn patience while they wait for

Mom to finish grocery shopping. They don't practice patience in restaurants while they wait for their food. Nor are children developing communication and coping skills within these situations because they would rather sedate themselves with the latest apps and games. Simply put, children no longer have to experience discomfort and boredom. Instead, they are pacified with a screen.

Children move from one pacifier to another as they grow up. Why? Because it makes life easier on us, the parents. Without realizing it, parents are enabling their child's dependence on screens which are known to rewire the brain, weaken eyesight, dilute purity, and ravage their ability to focus, among other things we are still discovering. The damage done to the frontal lobe of the brain when screens are excessively used during your child's formative years can mimic that of a neglected or abused child. In her book, Reset Your Child's Brain, Victoria Dunckly, MD, details what she calls Electronic Screen Syndrome (ESS).[11] The stress of excessive screen/media exposure to children produces biological, psychological, and social dysfunctions including:

- inability to plan, prioritize, and problem solve (executive functions)
- impulsive behavior
- mood swings, irritability, depression, anger
- difficulty learning, poor memory, inattention
- fight or flight/violent behavior
- impaired relationships: avoidance of eye contact, tendency to be competitive, defensive

Dr. Dunckly describes her first awareness of screen-time issues working with children from group homes, foster care, and even those who'd been adopted into families. At first she hypothesized the screen-time was exacerbating the already present psychological harm caused by neglect or abuse. Interestingly, her continued research found that children *without* any psychiatric diagnosis were just as likely to experience these negative effects.[12] The children raised in loving homes without a hint of neglect or abuse displayed the same negative outcomes from screens as the foster children. It was concluded that excessive screen-time damage is an equal opportunity predator to a developing brain.

This hit home for me as these ESS symptoms are all behaviors and dysfunctions I have seen in children from foster care whom have experienced trauma, abuse, and neglect. Could it be that neglect to a screen causes similar results as neglect from a parent? Living with these heartbreaking dysfunctions every day, I wouldn't wish them upon any child or parent. It saddens me to consider that all the children growing up with excessive screen-time today could produce a society of adults emotionally stunted and psychologically damaged by this new form of neglect.

The risks associated with pacifying our kids with screens are higher than we think. Neglect is a hard word to digest. Take a moment to reflect on whether you have ever found yourself using the screen to calm, soothe, or pacify. Have you "forgotten" about your children because they were well-behaved on their screen? Have you outsourced their learning to a screen? We must consider what is lost when relationships and life lessons are neglected and replaced by a screen.

Learning patience is a lifelong process and can be taught in a multitude of ways. Lessons in patience, while rarely pleasurable, are far easier to learn while the brain is still forming. Therefore, it is crucial parents begin teaching and requiring screen-related patience early on rather than when neurological pathways are already set against it. In other words, like it is hard to teach an old dog new tricks, it is hard to teach a screen-obsessed child healthy media habits.

Patience is not a battle to fight *against* your children. It is our battle to fight *for* our children. We need to fight the desire to pacify, soothe, comfort, and instruct with a device. We must contend with our own impatience and weaknesses. Our young children are not consciously making the choice to use or reject smart technology. We make the choice for them when we allow or withhold devices.

Do you have the patience to allow temporary unhappiness and discontentment? Do you have the patience to help your child develop healthy coping skills when trapped in the longest grocery line with the slowest cashier? Are you brave enough to force your child to verbally communicate to make new friends instead of hiding behind a screen? Can you say no to the 14+ rated gaming app for your seven-year-old when he begs you to say yes? Or the social media app your ten-year-old daughter assures you is just for making music videos, and all of her church friends have it (so surely it's okay)? Will you say no? What will you say when your child calls out the pacification directly, as my youngest did, "I'm just going to sit here and annoy you until you give me my iPod." Will you withstand the annoyance?

Are you brave enough to fight the necessary and brutal battles for your child's character in order to win the war?

NEED?

The propensity to give our kids *what they want* over what they *need* is a lack of patience on our part as parents. They *want* an iPad or iPhone; they don't *need* one. They *want* to play games on your phone while riding in the car; they don't *need* to.

Parents everywhere are scrambling to figure out what is an actual media or screen "need" and what is only a "want." In our haste, we make credulous assumptions that screens are *good* for our kids —

educational even. We like to act as though we have it all figured out, but we have to consider, maybe we don't!

Need:

noun

(1) a requirement, necessary duty, or obligation.

verb used without object

(2) to be under an obligation[13]

Consider the words "requirement" and "obligation." Is anything screen related a requirement? Are you required to have cable television at home? Do you require your child to play video games or watch YouTube every day? Are you under an obligation to keep your children updated with the latest and greatest phones on the market? No, no, and no.

THE PROPENSITY TO GIVE OUR KIDS WHAT THEY WANT OVER WHAT THEY NEED IS A LACK OF PATIENCE ON OUR PART AS PARENTS.

From a child's viewpoint, they can attempt to persuade you that it is a requirement: "My teacher told me I have to bring a phone or tablet to school so we can do research tomorrow," or "The only way I will ever make friends is if I have a smartphone — no one talks to people anymore. They only text!" Similarly, kids can try to guilt you into feeling obligated to buy that first smartphone: "I don't understand why you don't love me. If you really loved me, you would want me to be happy, and you know I'll be happy with a phone!" Ultimately, they should know it is a want, but the world convinces them a smartphone is a need.

So if we recognize there is no need, requirement, or obligation to provide our children with screens, and likewise, children have no imminent need for such things, *what is driving parents to hand screens over so willingly?*

Perhaps it stems from our wants that we justify as needs. We want them to be on screens in order to gain peace and quiet: An interruption-free lunch with a friend, making dinner without fifty questions, grocery shopping without tantrums, or maybe even time to indulge in our own screen habits. We want our children to be babysat by a screen while we run an errand or take a shower. We love when they are distracted and not begging us to play dolls or cars every 30 minutes. We cherish how little mess is made when they play Minecraft all day instead of playing with Lego® bricks or building forts. We love not dealing with our teenagers' attitudes and eye rolls when they spend their entire evenings inside their social media accounts. We love not having to parent when the screen is on. We want to keep them safe; therefore, we need to track their location at all times. We want the ability to contact them at any time of the day, so they need to have their phones at the ready while in school.

Our wants justified as needs.

Ouch, right? Many of us cannot deny this truth. Remember, I am not condemning you for having these thoughts and feelings. I, too, still wrestle with these ideas and emotions. So often, mostly during the summer, I think of all the wonderful benefits I would gain if I didn't care about screen-time. All of these sanity-saving and calm-cultivating promises tempt me day after day to give in to screens.

What makes fighting this temptation even harder is that we are contending against the very things our kids deeply and passionately desire. The pressure is enough to break the strongest of parents.

If screens make it easier on both the parent and child, why resist?

Why withhold a screen and make yourself and your child miserable?

Instead of tackling these tough questions, many take the easy way out and justify their wants as perceived benefits.

A survey done by Grunwald Associates, First Learning Initiative, and AT&T, *Living and Learning with Mobile Devices,*[14] identified parents' proclivity to allow young children's use of handheld devices. It revealed 85 percent of parents believe the devices made *learning* fun for their children. More than 75 percent believe these same devices promote curiosity and teach reading and math skills. Additionally, greater than 60 percent of parents surveyed feel mobile devices teach responsibility and problem solving to their children.

Imagine: one device that teaches a child to be curious, read more (and better), problem solve, and be responsible — who wouldn't buy this for their kid? It sounds amazing!

But wait, there's more! Not only do you get curiosity, reading improvement, problem solving and responsibility — but if you give in now you'll also get Peace and Quiet with zero distractions — all for Free! Don't delay, give in today!

This cheesy infomercial has relentlessly played in the hearts and minds of so many parents. Too many believe this is the best parenting deal ever.

Knowing this helps explain why, by the age of four, 64 percent of children have their own phone or device, according to a survey done by the American Academy of Pediatrics.[15]

Now for the fast, auctioneer-style verbal disclaimer at the end of our infomercial. The above study, *Living and Learning with Mobile Devices,* only identified the way parents perceive mobile devices. The study did not measure the effect of devices on curiosity, responsibility, or reading and math skills. Parents simply reported what they wanted to believe.

And it's easy to understand why. What parent would ever admit, "I gave my eight-year-old a device to make him dumb" or "I set my teenage daughter up to fail by allowing her to have whatever she wanted on her phone"? No one would admit that. We want to believe screens are beneficial — or at least neutral — so we can justify their use.

There are side effects of screen use we can no longer ignore. If you've watched any television in the past several years, you've surely seen a pharmaceutical drug commercial. Similar to our infomercial disclaimer, these commercials rapid-fire a list of potential and scary side effects they are required to disclose. Side effects such as *sudden cardiac arrest or extreme diarrhea and flatulence* truly require a person to weigh the risk versus reward of that drug. In the same way, parents must consider the side effects of prolific screen use to a child's life and character:

- Decreased empathy with lack of face-to-face (and voice-to-voice) communication,[16]
- Fewer deep relationships due to amassing casual contacts and connections driven by a culture of competition,[17]
- Decreased critical thinking and learning when every homework answer can be found on Google,[18]
- Self-aggrandizement in a generation who believe they deserve to be the next viral superstar for doing nothing of importance or of value,
- Shallow aspirations, dreams, and self-reflection due to over-connection and ceaseless availability, [19]
- Increased automobile accidents when teenagers cannot go fifteen minutes without using or checking their phones,[20]

32

- Poor sleeping habits in part because of lighted screens before bedtime and phone use throughout the night, [21]
- Heightened anxiety and feelings of loneliness due to perceived fear of missing out (FOMO),[22]
- Degraded purity, morals, and understanding of sexuality in a pornography-saturated and sex-promoting world,[23]
- Plummeted self-esteem and self-worth while living for the likes, follows, and verification from others on social media,[24]
- Addiction to gaming and social media, the new socially accepted drugs,[25] and
- Diminished focus and cognitive brain capacity in the mere presence of one's smartphone. [26]

Imagine if every advertisement for smartphones and devices included a deep voiced, speed talking announcer who listed these side effects out loud. Would we reconsider our desire to track their location or have them pacified during our lunch dates? In the same way pharmaceutical drugs prescribed in an open market leads to the discovery of unpredicted side effects and adverse reactions, our world is just beginning to discover the unpredicted side effects of excessive screen-time in young children.

I have yet to find a parent who believes YouTube increases her child's safety or that Instagram-filtered selfies builds strong character. If the primary reason parents give a device to their child is to contact them, know their location, and for education – why do they allow all the extra apps that aren't educational?

The truth, that we should all know but gets buried under consumerism, is that far greater ways exist to promote learning in our young children other than a screen. Reading to your child remains a superior method to develop reading comprehension compared to "edu-games" on devices. Responsibility and problem solving have been taught for generations without the existence of handheld screens.

But gigantic corporations like Google and Apple know how to sell their products and make millions by convincing parents "technology is the only way."

The first world problem at hand is our privilege leads to entitlement. Entitlement weaves its way through thoughts and morals, consuming patience, gratitude, and empathy on its destructive path. Entitlement is the enemy of patience.

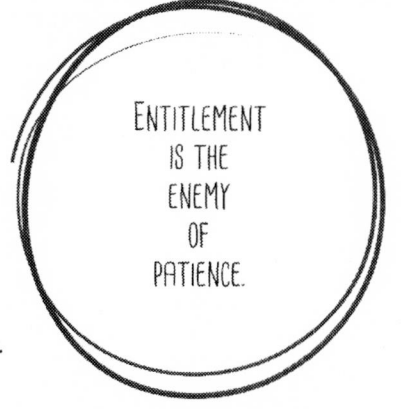

ENTITLEMENT IS THE ENEMY OF PATIENCE.

Children do not have an inherent need or right to phones or devices. Yes, we live in a society and time when we can afford this technology for our children, but to what gain? So they can take hundreds of selfies a day? Play Minecraft for hours? Participate in social media, YouTube stunts, and challenges in attempts to garner fame? Scroll through endless social media feeds absorbed in celebrities' lives instead of homework?

Therefore, keeping our eyes on the target of patience, the standard we will use to develop this characteristic is **Wait for the privilege**.

Wait until your child is old enough to handle small doses of screen-time.

Wait until a device is an earned privilege instead of pacification.

Wait for the privilege of all the extras (apps, games, internet, camera, etc.).

Wait for there to be an authentic need instead of a superficial want for a smartphone.

WHY WAIT?

We make them wait because instant and unlimited anything can breed obsession and addiction.

With the average first smart-phone ownership at age ten, it is estimated 50 percent of today's elementary-aged children have their own smartphones.[27] In 2012, Pew Research reported only 8 percent of children ages twelve to thirteen had their own smartphone.[28] We've gone from only 1-in-12 middle-school aged kids having a smartphone to 1-in-2 elementary-aged kids having them. Compared to other technological advances over the ages, this breakneck proliferation is unprecedented.

As we asked before, why not just given in? Why wait to give them a smartphone? It is what they want, and it is easier for parents. Because character is greater! Because the risks are real. Because patience is needed in us, just as much as it is needed in our children.

Let us not become weary in doing good, for at the proper time we will reap a harvest if we do not give up.

Galatians 6:9

Is *Waiting for the privilege* hard for the parent? Absolutely. You may feel like the last one standing, as the rest of society bows down in Babylonian-style worship to the new gold iPhone. Resisting conformity often feels like suffering.

...after you have suffered a little while, he will restore, support, and strengthen you, and he will place you on a firm foundation.

1 Peter 5:10 (NLT)

Is *Waiting for the privilege* hard for the child? You bet! Anything worth gaining takes hard work. It is through the hard struggles that patience, endurance, and strength of character are developed.

Because of our faith, Christ has brought us into this place of undeserved privilege where we now stand, and we confidently and joyfully look forward to sharing God's glory. We can rejoice, too, when we run into problems and trials, for we know that they help us develop endurance. And endurance develops strength of character, and character strengthens our confident hope of salvation.

Romans 5: 2-4 (NLT)

We are truly in a place of undeserved privilege. We must confidently parent our children to possess the character God desires.

Therefore, as God's chosen people, holy and dearly loved, clothe yourselves with compassion, kindness, humility, gentleness and patience.

Colossians 3:12

The most beautiful part of *Waiting for the privilege* is how God develops the character He desires in us as we develop it in our children. We are to be transformed by our calling to parent children. This doesn't happen by conforming to societal norms but by applying wisdom as Romans 12:2 states. Our flesh may say, "Give them a smartphone. It's what they want," but the Holy Spirit will say, "Seek first his kingdom and his righteousness, and all these things will be given to you as well." (Mat 6:33)

WAITING FOR THE PRIVILEGE OF SCREEN-TIME

Waiting for the privilege essentially starts when your child is born. When your child can make eye contact with you, they can make eye contact with a screen. When your child can hold a rattle or bottle, they can also hold a device. But should they?

The American Academy of Pediatrics (AAP) recommends no digital screen-time under the age of eighteen months old. This includes television, phones, tablets, and other devices. From age two to five, the recommendation is for only one hour per day of high-quality programming and co-viewed screen-time.[29]   The AAP has set these guidelines based on neurological, emotional, and behavioral science known about child development.

You may think this recommendation is impossible to uphold with today's digital dependence, but you cannot deny it is a goal worth striving for.

Infants

In order for your infant to *Wait for the privilege,* you must commit to not pacify or soothe with your phone, tablet, or television. The goal is zero screen-time for children under eighteen months. Also, you should not pass the time while caring for your infant by constantly gazing at your own screen. The attention you give your child matters tremendously.

Toddlers

For your toddler to *Wait for the privilege,* you must commit to only allowing high-quality programming. This isn't just any old app you find that holds their attention. You must also commit to co-view their screen-time to help them understand what they are watching. Devices are not adequate babysitters. Early screen-time habits build lifelong neurological pathways. These are not pathways leading to tech-savviness, but rather tech-dependence.

School-aged

Helping your school-aged child *Wait for the privilege* will look different as technology continues to permeate all aspects of education. Many schools are incorporating technology in everything they do: computerized reading testing, spelling tests on iPads, Google classroom, Edmodo, Prodigy, and so on. Because your child is likely to have screen-time at school, they are bound to desire more screen-time at home. Patience can be taught by waiting for the weekend for non-educational screen-time and through waiting for the privilege of downloading games and apps.

If the current trend of first smartphone ownership in fourth to fifth grade continues, you may find yourself contemplating a transition from device to smartphone earlier than you expected. Before making a decision, consider that to a child, having a phone means they have reached a pinnacle in their social and personal life. Regardless of how young and unassuming their social life seems, all of their relationships will change with owning a phone. With a phone in hand, there is *no need for parents* to arrange play dates, to search for that cute outfit or pair of shoes on a website, to look up when a movie is playing, or to take a picture. Children see themselves possessing the same level of autonomy and freedom as their parents.

This is freedom in a way we couldn't dream of when we were growing up pre-Internet. Possessing and using the same technology as every adult does deceives children into thinking it brings true independence. Rather, their smartphone use becomes bondage. It is the chains of constant connection and enslavement to immediate gratification, all of which is beyond what their brains can comprehend and their emotional health can endure.

As every parent who has given a smartphone to a child can attest: once you go there, you can never go back. The smartphone changes their behaviors, emotions, and character.

Therefore, before you cave in to your child's "need" for a smartphone, you must weigh the cost versus reward. Although not every user experiences the side effects, they are certainly well documented.

Children deserve a childhood, not a smartphone. Our patience gives them untethered time to grow and mature as they *Wait for the privilege.*

THE SMARTPHONE

After your child has practiced patience waiting for a phone or device, he can continue honing this quality through phone standards and expectations.

We will use two smartphone standards to build patience. Although we primarily discuss smartphones here, these rules are applicable and essential for any media method: phone, tablet, video games, or computers.

The first rule is *Limited Access* to the smartphone.

Unfortunately, few concrete recommendations and standards have been set for older adolescents and teens regarding digital screen-time. This both enables and requires parents to establish boundaries and guidelines. This parental responsibility to set healthy limits has been left in the dust of mobile technology's rapid proliferation and acceptance.

The *Limited Access* to a smartphone rule is the foundation to develop healthy use rather than obsessive use. This means a child cannot carry the phone around at all times. The now common practice of having the phone in hand or nearby at all times perpetuates the "always on/always available" mind-set, which breeds addictive habits.

A recent survey revealed 76 percent of smartphone users are no more than five feet from their smartphones at any time of the day.[30] Most especially during the first year or two of phone ownership, this rule helps children recognize the phone for its primary purpose of communication rather than its entertainment value.

We must model this standard for our young children who watch and learn from our every move. When we practice *Limited Access*, such as using our phones only at certain times and places, we demonstrate to our children the ability and importance of patience through digitally disconnected time. If we use our smartphones nearly 24/7, we can absolutely expect our children will do the same.

Create a designated place in the home where the phone is stored and kept, then establish boundaries for where the phone can be used. For example, it may be used for football practice or going to the movies with friends when parents won't be present. Also, define when the smartphone can be used at home, such as during designated screen-time hours or with a parent's permission. Ultimately, *Limited Access* means the phone isn't carried around in the back pocket 24/7.

The second rule for the privilege of using a smartphone is *Limited Usage* through the application of parental restrictions.

Smartphones come with robust sets of apps pre-installed at the time of purchase. Most of these features are completely unnecessary for your child and should be disabled. Whether the smartphone is Apple or Android based, both allow for strong parental restrictions essentially turning off everything "smart." The web browser, social media platforms, camera, and games are features your child can earn.

This serves to reinforce why they have a phone — so they can contact you and vice versa, not so they can begin consuming six to nine hours of digital media per day. Allowing this time to acclimate to having a phone without the allure of unnecessary apps can reduce the instantly addictive properties. As your child matures and demonstrates positive and responsible smartphone behavior, you can begin to enable more apps and features.

The obvious key to *Limited Usage* is not to give 100 percent access 100 percent of the time, as this is the antithesis of patience. Not only will your child develop patience waiting for and earning features, but they will also learn appreciation and respect. We'll discuss respect further in the next chapter.

Patience is not a onetime lesson; it is a constant practice, an ongoing struggle. *Limited Access* and *Limited Usage* can help you and your child develop this virtue and gain healthier habits in the process.

CHAPTER TWO

Respect:
Boundaries for everyone

Nearly all men can stand adversity, but if you want to test a man's character, give him power. [31]

Abraham Lincoln

When I entered college in the fall of 1996, the University of Kentucky promptly issued me my first .edu email address. In absolute technological ignorance, I sent my first email to a friend, typing everything in the Subject line. I hadn't grown up in a home with computers, so my highest level of technology usage was an electric typewriter. When I met my husband in 1999, he was the most tech-advanced person I knew. His entire life seemed to revolve around computers and technology, not to mention he was the only person I knew who owned a DVD player. Oh, how times have changed!

During our first year of dating, my first year of Pharmacy school, he bought me my very own laptop. I know, pretty generous boyfriend, right? At the time, I lived in a sorority house with two computers to be shared among fifty women. I had to walk ten minutes to the nearest computer lab. Having a computer of my own was a *dream*! Ryan taught me new things every day. As my understanding of it grew, so did my love for working on my computer.

One day, while chugging away on my hardest class at the time, biochemistry, I leaned across my desk for a book. The corner of my elbow connected perfectly with my full glass of sweet tea. I watched in horrified shock as the sugar-laden liquid covered over and then disappeared under the keys of my brand-new laptop. I stood paralyzed and clueless as to how I should react. When I snapped out of my shock, I tipped the entire laptop upside down in an attempt to drain the sweet tea from under the keys. As I feverishly shook it, I heard it breathe its final sigh before its death. And then I silently wished for my own death.

How on earth was I going to explain this to Ryan — the man I was still only dating, who had once discussed wanting to marry me, but now, surely, would he change his mind? A thousand apologies would not forgive my disrespect for his money spent and the technology with which he trusted me. I wanted to run away, crawl into a hole, or just die — anything but face his disappointment.

I cannot remember how I told him (although I'm fairly certain I shed tears and babbled that it was okay if he didn't want to marry me anymore). I do remember with great clarity his forgiving response. After he looked over the laptop, he took a deep breath and with loving compassion he said, "Computers and iced tea don't go together, Kel. Now you know."

We made several attempts to repair the laptop over the next several months, but we finally conceded to having a quiet funeral and putting the situation behind us. Amazingly, and to my own astonishment, we were engaged later that month.

My respect for technology and my fiancé turned husband made giant strides over the next three years. From dial-up Internet when we began dating to my first cell phone in 2001 after we were married, I'd learned a lot. But Ryan and I both knew that I needed boundaries regarding tech devices. Neither of us wanted to repeat the Great Iced Tea Incident of 1999.

Like many other parents, I learned to respect technology as a young adult. As I chose to adapt to advancements in technology — and by "adapt" I mean forced along by my high-tech husband — I always recognized the power these computers and phones held over me. These devices were smarter and more powerful than I would ever be, and for that reason alone, they deserved my respect.

Now, two decades later, our children are teaching *us* new technology. Our children aren't adapting to technological advancements; this is the only way of life they know. Babies can now effectively use technology before speaking full sentences. Toddlers absorb neurologically altering media as fast as the processors can relay it. Adolescents learn how video games eliminate boredom, while granting them a sense of control and escape. Tweens join the social media movement, transforming their small circle of influence into a global field of connections. And teenagers everywhere are so emotionally dependent on their phones, they don't even realize they have lost the ability to communicate.

As a result of these global and cultural technology shifts, children have learned new behaviors:

- disruptive behavior while Dad works from home may equal extra screen-time,
- a gigantic tantrum in a busy grocery store will get me Mom's iPhone to play with,

- making new friends is awkward, so I'll just look at my phone so no one talks to me,
- why be bored when there are tons of fun apps to play, and
- visual stimulation feels good, so I think I'll keep going all night.

The combination of increased screen-time, media consumption, and the corresponding behavioral changes are fundamentally altering the way we communicate and relate to one another. Relationships are suffering due to technology nullifying the need for respect. Respect is the foundation of every relationship, whether it be parent/child, boss/employee, teacher/student, or friend/friend.

In the past, respect was a valuable currency for successful and enjoyable relationships, both business and personal. For children today, however, their social currency is technology itself. Who has the latest and greatest smartphone? Who's on what social media accounts? How many followers do you have? How many likes do your selfies get? Who has access to pornography? What is your longest snap streak? Who has the most nudes saved on their camera roll? Sadly, these are some of the qualifications to establish popularity. The foundation of respect is cracked by these powerful, deep-rooted beliefs of how their social world works. Without a solid foundation, relationships crumble.

It's easy for us as parents to see this sweeping problem in our children's relationships, but repairing it is something quite different. It will require intensive, intentional action and, of course, bravery.

The standard we will use to build and maintain respect is ***Boundaries for everyone.***

BUT FIRST, US

As parents, we often buy into the idea that we can be a parent *as well as* our child's best friend. This may not be news to you but maybe you aren't aware of the cost. A "best friends" relationship with your child costs respect. The less we parent, teach, and discipline our children (because that isn't what best friends do), the less respect they will have for our role as parents. All parents desire to be respected by their children, but to gain this, we must live and act like parents — not best friends.

First and foremost, we must look at our own behaviors. Regarding smartphone and media habits, we must acknowledge that respect is earned rather than automatically granted. A father constantly on his phone cannot tell his teenage daughter to get off her phone because it is unhealthy. The old mantra "Do as I say, not as I do" does not hold up in our overly connected world. The parent must model respectful behavior to earn respect.

What does respectful behavior look like for a parent?

- Do you talk, text, or search while checking out at the grocery store, walking through the mall, or during dinner at a restaurant?
- Do you continue a text conversation while your child rambles on about her school day?
- Do you aimlessly tap through Instagram or Facebook while your child does his homework?
- Do you use your phone while driving, ignoring the general safety of other motorists?
- Do you lose track of time in the rabbit hole of news, maybe forgetting to pick up your child from baseball practice?
- Are you taking (and retaking) dozens of pictures, ensuring your kids look perfect for your next post?

Perhaps these few examples do not seem like disrespectful behaviors to *you*. Now, insert your child's name into the above questions. Chances are, these behaviors from your child would be considered disrespectful.

Do you find yourself trying to justify these types of behaviors, but in your spirit you recognize you've slipped into complacency with your own media behavior? Self-reflection is hard and sometimes painful. It requires self-discipline to escape this complacency. Discipline doesn't *feel* good — for us or our children — but we *know* it is good.

Or have you forgotten how good parents treat children, and that God regards you as his children? My dear child, don't shrug off God's discipline, but don't be crushed by it either. It's the child he loves that he disciplines; the child he embraces, he also corrects. God is educating you; that's why you must never drop out. He's treating you as dear children. This trouble you're in isn't punishment; it's training, the normal experience of children. Only irresponsible parents leave children to fend for themselves. Would you prefer an irresponsible God? We respect our own parents for training and not spoiling us, so why not embrace God's training so we can truly live? While we were children, our parents did what seemed best to them. But God is doing what is best for us, training us to live God's holy best. At the time, discipline isn't much fun. It always feels like it's going against the grain. Later, of course, it pays off handsomely, for it's the well-trained who find themselves mature in their relationship with God.

Hebrews 12:9-11 (MSG)

Parents, we must embrace training and discipline ourselves to develop and model respectful phone and media behavior. This training is done through God's word and through relevant application, such as this book. We are the adults — the parents. We've lived long enough to know that discipline is good. We must be responsible parents who train their children *and themselves*. We are not above reproach. Smartphones and social media have affected our own character as much as our children's. Whether you are guilty of using your smartphone when you should be engaged with your child, allowing the screen to pacify and entertain, or oversharing pictures of your child, allow God's grace and mercy to cover your best efforts and intentions up to this point. Right now is the time to awaken, accept training, implement boundaries, and discipline yourself, so your child can do the same.

THE PARENT MUST MODEL RESPECTFUL BEHAVIOR TO EARN RESPECT.

One of the best ways to monitor how your media behavior affects others is through accountability. We'll discuss accountability over and over throughout the upcoming chapters regarding keeping our children accountable, but it is of equal benefit to us as well. Ideally your accountability partner will be your spouse, but if you are a single parent or a parent struggling to find common ground with your spouse as you manage media, choose someone with whom you spend the most quality time. This could even be your child! Nothing is more authentic and vulnerable than admitting to your child that you need help managing media — much less that you are still learning and still being disciplined by God.

Whoever you choose to hold you accountable, grant them permission to evaluate your habits and give correction immediately. Give them grace and don't get mad at them for doing what you asked. Accept their insight and wisdom throughout, knowing God is honored by your commitment to living His holy best. Above all, allow your accountability partner to be honest without your judgment. This isn't an opportunity for you to justify behaviors. You need honest critique — even if you don't want it — in order to be a positive role model of respectable media behavior.

Some behaviors to ponder:

- Am I listening (truly *listening*) to others while still texting?
- Am I aimlessly looking at social media or watching television instead of engaging with the kids or my spouse?
- Do I waste time playing games or reading blogs while important tasks remain undone?
- Is my free time filled with phone time, whether in restaurants, at traffic lights, or to avoid social interactions?
- Am I venting emotions or frustrations on Facebook that should probably be left unsaid?
- Am I oversharing details of my child's life online which may come back to haunt or hurt them as an adult?
- Is the phone always in my hand? Or am I leaving it behind, allowing for unattached time?

The most common behavior we must all work to correct is phone snubbing, or "phubbing," as it is called. Yes, children today are notorious for looking at their phone pretending to be engaged to avoid interactions with others. Consider who they learned this from. Parents have loved the freedom a smartphone brings since the moment they hit the market. While our children watched, we've used (and abused) this freedom over the past ten years to work (check email, texts, and pay bills) and to play (games, browse social media, and shopping).

The irony of phubbing is how annoying we consider this behavior from modern youth, yet we continue to do it ourselves. If we can decrease how often we are on our smartphones in front of our children, regardless of their age, we can begin to shift the cultural norm back towards respecting the relationships we share a physical presence with.

Place restrictions on your own phone or computer — have your accountability partner set the password, turn your phone completely off, close social media accounts, and make new rules for yourself — whatever it takes! These boundaries are for your own good as much as it is your children's.

Humble yourself, confident that your vulnerability and self-discipline will lead to beneficial change. We cannot afford to be flippant regarding the respect we model every day. Rather, we must be intentional and vulnerable enough to realign our behaviors.

RESPECT THE TECH

One definition of respect is "to admire (someone or something) deeply as a result of their abilities, qualities, or achievements."[32] By this definition, children today definitely respect media and technology. Many would even say their admiration looks more like worship or, sadly, addiction.

A second definition is "a feeling or understanding that someone or something is important, serious, and should be treated in an appropriate way."[33] This definition, contrary to the former, is how our children should view media and technology. It is serious and something to be treated appropriately.

We are not playing with Playskool phones purchased with Monopoly money. These are high-powered and high-dollar devices, deserving great respect. A Google search can return porn as easily as it can return puppies. An eleven-year-old can wreck a smartphone as easily as a sixteen-year-old can wreck a Lamborghini. A nude picture sent to one classmate can virally infect an entire school just as fast as a Facebook video with a mom in a Chewbacca mask can go viral across the world.

Purchasing the latest smartphone for your child will not earn you respect. If this were true, wouldn't we have the most earnestly respectful generation in existence? Granting permission for numerous social media accounts where thousands of followers gather to see your daughter's perfected selfies is not respecting her self-worth. Giving access to unfiltered, unlimited, and unmonitored internet use does not propagate respect for purity in romantic relationships.

As we handle technology with respect, carefully considering how its use can affect character while managing its power in an appropriate way, our children will likewise learn to do the same. It will not be instantaneous, but as they watch the character of their peers crumble, crash, and cave, understanding will grow even more.

There are three types of technology-related respect we will focus on: self-respect, parental-respect, and respect for others. These areas, much like patience, establish a foundation for good character and healthy relationships amidst our digital dependence.

Self-Respect

It's almost unfair how quickly self-respect can be lost compared to how long it takes to build up. A young girl with straight A's and an impressive high school resume caves when her boyfriend of three months threatens to break up with her because she's boring.

Desperate, she takes a quick topless picture to send to him to prove she is worth keeping. He ends the relationship a short while later and shares her nude picture with his friends.

This one moment in time, captured and shared with one and then with many, can completely bankrupt her self-respect in a viral second. Finding or rediscovering this self-respect could take years or even a lifetime. The virtue of self-respect may seem all but lost with the pervasiveness of pornography, social media, and constant connectedness. Despite mass media touting a message of "no shame," shame isn't something we consciously decide to feel. Shame, which is bred and spread in the secret places of the Internet, is self-respect's greatest enemy. Shame quickly gives way to condemnation, and condemnation transforms hope into despair. Unfortunately, even a drop of shame can pollute an entire body of self-respect. However, shame is avoidable. Our role as parents is to ensure self-respect isn't lost in the dangerous waters of shame. This is why we must use the center point of their lives, the technology they love, to enforce and protect self-respect!

If you are diligently working to build self-respect in your child by establishing values and teaching forgiveness, hard work, and healthy self-care, you must recognize that not all parents will do the same for their children. Without intentional choice and action by parents, developing this character trait is left to peer influence and the culture at large.

We cannot allow our sons and daughters to be deceived. We must not abdicate our job of teaching our children the right kind of respect. If we do, our "anything goes" culture will gladly do the teaching. Victoria's Secret will define for our sons and daughters what self-respecting women look like, professional athletes will teach our young men that arrogance is a form of self-respect, and the feminism movement's popular celebrities will teach girls they can do and say anything as an expression of self-respect.

When all of this translates into twelve-year-olds stripping in front of web-cams, thirteen-year-old boys absorbed in hard core pornography, and fifteen-year-old girls giving oral sex on school buses, shame is the end result, not self-respect. Sexual sin never results in self-respect.

Respecting potential dangers means we establish appropriate boundaries. Parents must assume natural curiosity will prevail when children have unrestricted internet access and social media accounts.

When our children are babies and learning to crawl and then walk, we put up boundaries to protect them. We install cabinet locks to keep babies away from cleaning supplies and chemicals. We set up gates to block staircases. We take these safety measures because we know small children do not perceive the actual danger cleaning products and stairs pose. Natural curiosity compels them toward these potentially harmful novelties. Parents perceive the danger and thus secure boundaries for their babies' protection.

Likewise, children do not perceive inconsequential fame or popularity-seeking and irrational behavior on social media platforms as dangerous. But like a staircase, no boundaries allow our children to harm themselves. Natural curiosity draws them in, and all too quickly, they are tumbling down the staircase. The fall on a media platform may not lead to physical harm; however, emotional, mental, and spiritual harm is often present. Shame, regret, self-loathing, and self-harm are the common side effects in the wake of the technology fall.

A common scenario is a young girl who posts a provocative selfie to social media. She doesn't fully respect the range and reach one seductive picture can have. She has been given no boundaries, so her brain and conscience reason that this action must be okay. The picture, once released on social media, can be a catalyst for sexual bullying or shaming from peers, attract sex traffickers or child pornographers around the world, and remain in cyberspace to later resurface and haunt her reputation. This is where shame is born — partly because respect for the technology used was absent and partly because no boundaries were put in place for protection.

SEXUAL SIN NEVER RESULTS IN SELF-RESPECT.

How do you teach, establish, and maintain this level of self-respect along with a respect for technology? It begins early, when your child is a toddler. Limiting access and usage while encouraging other physically and mentally stimulating activities can keep screen-time in proper place.

When they are an age of understanding (but at the latest elementary school), begin age-appropriate conversations about the positive and negative aspects of the Internet and social media. It cannot be a *"The Internet is bad, don't use it. The end."* lesson. Children must understand there are both good and evil found within URLs, but you are there to guide them through to the good and away from the evil.

Additionally, to establish and maintain respect when they are of an age that requires use of devices, phones, or the Internet, you must erect boundaries for their protection. Having limited access to websites, social media, and texting until a child is ready and responsible can spare them from harmful, humiliating, or even self-defaming situations.

Constructing appropriate boundaries for your child's media use demands that you have a general knowledge of every app, game, program, website, etc. and its function before allowing its use. If you do not know what it is or how to use it — don't allow it!

It can be hard to keep current with these things; however, if you are implementing what you learned in the last chapter on patience, your child waits for you to be ready to allow something. Your patience, and thus their delay, is a boundary that helps build their self-respect.

Finally, when you consider what you will allow — whether a game, movie, or social media platform — take into account both boundaries and self-respect. Could the social media platform she wants lead her down a path where she does something to cause regret or shame? Could the online video games he wants to play lead him to aggressive or explosive behavior and a consequent loss of respect? Whether the potential is high or low, communicate the possibilities with them. Explain your understanding of the platform or game and why the need for boundaries exists. If you don't know enough to make a decision, admit it. Ask for their patience until you can learn more, and then decide whether it will be allowed. Please, I urge you, do not only give a "because I said so" answer, as this is counterproductive to growing their respect and understanding for the standard. It doesn't foster a healthy respect for you as their parent either.

Respect for Parents

As parents, we yearn for our children's respect. We don't need to feel guilty about this desire. It is God's design for the parent-child relationship. The biblical command for children to honor and obey their parents helps build respect; however, as we previously established regarding media and technology, we must also *earn respect*.

Parental-respect is not earned through caving in and granting the child's desires but rather through maintaining boundaries and consistent discipline.

In our parental fantasies, we like to assume we have automatic respect, considering we pay for the phone and its monthly bills. But reality tramples on these fantasies of ours. Whether its entitlement or shifts in our cultural norms, children today believe it is their inherent right to have a phone, and respect is owed to no one. We can alter this belief by the values, teaching, and modeling we cultivate in our home.

If we expect accountable and respectful behavior from our children, we must also display this standard in our own lives. Our own life circumstances do not allow the freedom to vacillate between strong convictions and habits one week and lackluster behavior the next. Personal accountability doesn't happen when it's personally convenient. We must consistently hold ourselves to the same expectations we hold our children to.

The majority of parents, myself included, falter when it comes to consistency and follow-through. Most parents start strong and operate with the standard, "If my child wants to use the device, they do so with my rules." Often these rules are general and are sifted through a filter of naïveté. Parents don't always know the trends of the teenage subculture and what type of boundaries are needed. They explain the rules, but all too quickly, discipline and consistency fatigue sets in. Couple this parental lethargy with the renewed free time and peaceful quiet that results from children being occupied with devices, and the original standard and expectations disintegrates.

Children seize this opportunity to shift the standard to their favor. They approach you for screen-time when you are exhausted and have had a terrible day, knowing your exacerbation will lead to a yes. Why? Because they know you want peace and quiet. This is not because they are bad children or because they disrespect you — although it may feel this way — but because the lure of screens is too good! With every concession deviating from the original rule and standard, the rules lose their strength. Gained in their place are manipulative respect and media dependency.

Our goal is to avoid the loss of parental respect by our own negligence and ignorance. Whatever standard you establish must be consistently maintained. In other words, don't make up rules you cannot follow yourself or hold your child accountable to. In the same way, don't allow them to use an app or game you don't know or understand. The standard practice and boundaries you establish should allow your child to grow toward greater freedom and less limitations as they demonstrate character. Start strict; relax when appropriate.

It would be foolish for us to discount how manipulative and persistent children can be when they want something. This isn't necessarily because they don't respect themselves or their parents. Human nature dictates curiosity, and the flesh often demands satisfaction. Even more, novelty is like a drug to the brain; the reward and satisfaction of discovering something new can drive adolescents beyond parental boundaries. Whether children find a way to hack around safety measures and boundaries you've put in place because they are assiduously curious or because they have nothing better to do, parents must be aware of and prepared for this likelihood.

This is not how the majority of the world are raising their children in regard to media. Therefore, this discipline may not feel good for you or your child. We must remember, this "isn't punishment; its training." This is the training that "always feels like it's going against the grain." But as the writer of Hebrews tells us, "later, of course, it pays off handsomely." (Hebrews 12:11)

Respect for Others

Because media and technology permeate all we do, from business to relationships, we cannot lose sight of the importance of respect for others. The respect children learn now will be the respect they display as adults. Our children may not be managing business transactions, but their relational transactions should be steeped in respect for the other person. Our focus now is to cultivate respect-building opportunities through relational transactions.

The truth we aim to instill is this: respect is won with intentionality and lost with impulsivity. A hand-written thank you note shows intentional gratitude and respect toward someone, where an impulsive text message with heated words demonstrates disrespect and uncontrolled emotions. The earlier we establish this concept as a foundation for how our children communicate and interact with peers, siblings, teachers, coaches, and bosses, the easier their relationships will be.

When phones and social media are added to the daily mix, our communication about what respectful behavior looks like must become crystal clear. The world at large has twisted and blurred the line of acceptable speech and behavior online and over phones. Our directives and expectations must be clearly defined statements of how to behave and how to communicate in a respectful way to others.

Let's begin with respect for the opposite sex. After all, this is the crux of tweens' and teens' existence.

Children are learning that respect isn't needed or important in relationships with the opposite sex. Boys learn through advertisements, video games, and movies that girls are merely objects pleasing to the eye. Grand Theft Auto IV, a popular video game among boys, allows players to have sex with a prostitute, then run her over with a car, beat her with a bat, or shoot her. As if that isn't bad enough, the player can then get their money back and find another prostitute and repeat the process.

Girls are taught that sexually forward and promiscuous behavior empowers them. This is seen through the sexual and sensual selfies posted on social media garnishing the most likes and followers. Articles headlined in magazines like Cosmopolitan, "Be His Best Sex Ever!"[34] or "Teach a Guy to Please YOU!"[35] work to further pollute our young girls' views of how they should be respected and give respect.

Parents — not the media — must teach respect until their children are mature enough to value this virtue themselves. Our boys must be diligently taught and shown how to properly respect women. Our girls, receiving the same confusing cultural messages through the media, need to be taught and shown how to respect themselves, as well as how to show proper respect for men. These conversations will likely be awkward but they are non-negotiable.

This specifically means we teach our sons never to ask, persuade, or blackmail a girl for nude pictures. Text conversations should never contain anything resembling a romance novel or porn script. His words should be intentionally respectful, assuming the girl's father or grandfather will always be reading what he writes.

In the same fashion, we teach our girls never to solicit attention through provocative or seductive pictures, videos, or texts. Impulsively texting "just got out of the shower" or "just lying on my bed" may seem harmless to innocent minds, but it can lead boys' hormone driven minds down a hyper-sexualized path. Likewise, if they have a social media account, it will be undeniably tempting to post that pop-star-like seductive photo (eyes deeply searching, cleavage showing, and lips plumped) in order to garnish more likes.

This is where we must teach them that attention received through this type of solicitation is not intentionally respectful to themselves or others.

For both boys and girls primarily communicating through text (where verbal and non-verbal cues are absent), your continual guidance is necessary. Provocative and pornographic communication is not the foundation for respectful relationships — even if they are culturally accepted and typical adolescent behavior. Check their texts to keep them accountable. Too many parents find it easier to ignore this reality and act like their sons and daughters are different. *(If they have hormones, they are no different.)*

Not only must we teach this virtue with clear directives and healthy boundaries, we should limit the type of behaviors lacking respect for others while our children grow up. Standards to prevent, protect, and build respect for others can include:

- Inability to send and receive pictures over text messages.
- Time restrictions for texting and internet use.
- Restricted access to social media sites.
- Proper filters and monitoring software to track computer use.
- Prohibited viewing of R-rated or sexually charged television shows and movies.

We'll go deeper into many of these standards in the succeeding chapters. For now, consider what intentional decisions you can make to help respectful character grow.

Finally, of increasing importance in our culture is the respect shown to others in public places while using our smartphones. Our society has completely sold out to smartphones. No longer do people seek the smartphone to be more efficient in their everyday tasks; now they seek out new things they can do in order to use their phone more. With nearly half of all Americans reporting they check their phone before arising out of bed in the morning and as the last thing they do before falling asleep at night,[36] smartphone usage isn't our second nature anymore, but our first.

Conversations over coffee, a meal, or even during a brief encounter at the grocery store all stand in constant competition with our smartphones. One buzz or ring compels you to abandon your face-to-face conversation to see if something better is happening on the phone. This is the phubbing behavior mentioned earlier in this chapter. Although socially prevalent and normalized, it is disrespect in action. As we work to realign our own phubbing habits, we can work to establish healthy habits with our children as well.

Recently, I experienced this disrespect during my "day job" as a retail pharmacist. I sat down in my immunization room with a mother and her two sons, ages twelve and nine, to administer their yearly flu vaccines. The twelve-year-old boy volunteered to go first and as I approached his arm with the needle, his phone rang. Abruptly, he stood up and said, "I've got to take this." He opened the door to walk out while I sat completely awestruck by his actions with an exposed needle still in my hand. I turned toward the mother, who laughed at first, but then called her son back into the room after seeing my facial expression.

Just because smartphones allow for on-demand connection, doesn't mean a child needs it or will flourish with it. Respecting others, whether it be adults or peers, is an imperative lesson for a child's success. It must be taught, practiced, and expected in every place, whether public or private.

Respecting others in public places requires healthy habits of moderation and presence (also known in our culture as mindfulness).

Pre-commit to healthy boundaries in order to build habits of moderation with your child's smartphone. Include yourself in these expected habits:

- no walking while texting,
- no phones at (or on) the dinner table or in the car,
- no social media checking, news scrolling, or texting when someone is speaking,
- no talking on the phone or texting in check-out lines or waiting rooms, and
- phones belong in pocket or purse/bag when not used (not in your hand).

Learning moderation enables you to ignore a text buzz while enjoying coffee with a friend or resist scrolling through Pinterest for the few minutes you wait in line at a store. When we practice moderation, we have the ability to show respect to others around us. Respect can be found in eye contact, two-way conversations, attention, patience, and self-control. The more moderation is expected and practiced, the more naturally present and respectful your child can be in public spaces.

HOW MUCH WILL YOUR CHILDREN MISS IF THEY ARE GROWING UP LOOKING DOWN?

The beautiful byproduct of moderation is *presence*. This allows you and your child to see the world not just through pictures, but to experience its beauty with all senses. Presence also grants access to the people God ordained to be near: family, friends, teachers, the random stranger who needs a smile, or the struggling soul in need of help. Presence gives the ability to be the hands and feet of Jesus! Additionally, presence gives the brain needed downtime to process, reflect, and meditate. How much will your children miss if they are growing up looking down?

You can give the gift of presence by resisting — that is, not allowing — unlimited and obsessive use everywhere your child goes. Teenagers may say, "I don't want that gift — I'd rather have a social media "presence" than be present with people I don't like or care about."

This is only their naiveté speaking. Relationships free from the pressure of ceaseless connection are a gift. Our children just don't understand it because they haven't experienced it. It is our job to lead them to the present of presence.

We cannot separate teaching respect from the technology children crave. It begins with us. Our intentionality, our accountability, and our standard won't feel good at the time, but later they will pay dividends. If it feels awkward, uncomfortable, and like you are going against the grain of culture as you build respect, chances are, you're on the right track.

CHAPTER THREE

Kindness:

Read what they type; coach what they say

*Kindness is the language which the deaf can hear
and the blind can see.* [37]

Mark Twain

After we adopted our first two children in 2008, we took a hiatus from the emotionally daunting world of foster care. But by 2010, I was confident we were not finished adopting children. I fearlessly told my husband, "Our family is missing one child." Unsure what this would look like, we prayed and waited.

In 2011, amidst our recent calling to drastically downsize our home, simplify our lifestyle, start a nonprofit, as well as my husband beginning seminary, I was still certain we would add more members to our family. We admittedly enjoyed life as a family of four; it was manageable as parents. However, the calling was getting louder and by 2012, we both knew we could not ignore God's nudge to adopt again. On a Saturday morning in January 2013, we arrived at our foster agency's ranch ready to retake our licensing classes.

We begrudged the need for two full days of training in order to be relicensed as foster parents. Remembering how useless and painfully boring our first licensing classes were six years prior had me wishing a middle-of-the-night stomach virus would take me out for the day. However, to my absolute surprise and delight, our instructor did not read to us from a manual on parenting kids from trauma, as our first had years ago. Instead, heartbreaking stories flowed, holding my attention captive. Her passion for foster children was so rich, her heart overflowed with stories. In the most beautiful, yet amazingly unrehearsed way, she told one story after another of traumatized children and how they were redeemed through parents willing to love them despite their past.

Waves of conviction ripped through my personal parenting record book, revealing how ill- prepared and ill-equipped I actually was to raise children from hard places. I became acutely aware that the success and redemption my two children were experiencing was a result of God's grace far more than my parenting.

I committed in that moment to listen and learn from this woman, a sage who seemingly knew the key to redeeming the lives of children from foster care. She stood confidently in front of our group, holding her very squirmy, infant foster son, while we sat comfortably soaking in her wisdom. She wasn't giving specific instructions such as, "Be sure to have a good counselor or therapist who takes Medicaid," or even precise tactics like, "Time-outs make them feel even more isolated, so use punishments like early bedtimes when they need to face a consequence." In this session, she rarely mentioned practical strategies at all. Instead, she spoke of only one key factor to both our success as foster parents and redemption of our children:

Kindness.

She emphasized the word over and over again. *Kindness.* Through every story she shared, she related how kindness had led to the child's redemption. I was in awe. Could it be this easy? I was desperate to find out.

During our active participation segment of the training, the instructor divided us into groups and gave each group a scenario. We were instructed to act out our scenario and show how kindness could change the outcome. While I generally detest role-playing, I can humbly admit that this process changed my entire way of thinking.

When it was my group's turn to demonstrate our scenario for the class, I was designated to act as the "parent." It was my job to convey kindness to the "child" who was, in our scenario, "dressing slutty for school." As I owned my part as the "kind parent," I instantly knew there was something extremely powerful in acting this out. With forethought, I was able to deliberately choose my words and filter them through kindness. My deliberately kind words helped transform the scenario from one of anger, disgust, and frustration to one of kindness and resolution. If the same or a similar scenario played out in real life — without any forethought as to how I'd respond — I can assure you, my reaction would not have been kind.

When we left the ranch that day, we took renewed and changed hearts toward parenting and showing kindness. It wasn't that I didn't acknowledge, attempt, or count kindness as valuable in our home, because I was sure I did. This was wholly different. I saw kindness as the answer to the question I didn't even know how to ask before this day. Kindness is a parenting strategy, a relationship method, an enemy resister, a selfishness fighter, and most of all, a choice.

KINDNESS GROWS

When God our Savior revealed his kindness and love,
he saved us, not because of the righteous things we had
done, but because of his mercy. He washed away our
sins, giving us a new birth and new life through the
Holy Spirit.

Titus 3:4-5 (NLT)

Whether we are parenting biological, foster, or adopted children, we are to reveal the love and kindness of Christ Jesus through our relationship with and training of our children. Kindness has to play a key role not only in how we live and parent, but also in how we train our children to act.

Kindness must be intentional in order to reveal Christ's redeeming love. For people who did not grow up with kind parents, influences, or circumstances and who struggle to grasp and accept God's kindness, this may not come naturally, but it can be learned. However, it must first be chosen.

Living as a kind parent requires you to make the simple, every day decision to act kindly. I choose to act kindly because my children need to learn how to treat others kindly. My choice of kindness isn't in return for their kindness or because of their accomplishments. Likewise, I don't withhold kindness when they are unkind to me. This is the mercy, love, and kindness we receive from Jesus and model for our children. Since we are not granted God's kindness based on our own worthiness, we must parent with the same undeserved kindness. When we mimic our heavenly father, setting the standard for kindness, we plant seeds which grow and reproduce more kindness in the lives of our children.

As any parent knows, kindness can sometimes be hard in the moment (imagine seven loud children all fighting over something — you know my struggle). Therefore, it's helpful to choose kind acts to do every day. Intentional kindness can be as easy as greeting your children joyfully and attentively every day, inviting them to be a part of whatever you are doing, listening intently to their stories, making their favorite meals, playing games with them, reading stories together, fixing their hair, valuing their opinion, and so on.

Kindness is a decision.

Children will continuously be transformed by kindness through your natural interactions with them. In addition, you can also promote and teach kindness through your child's storytelling. Listen to their stories and look for opportunities to point out kindness or ask questions about how kindness could have changed the story. After school or at dinner, ask if anyone showed them kindness or if they showed kindness to someone else. Discuss how kind (and unkind) responses affect friendships and their feelings toward others. Share a story of your own where someone's kindness positively impacted you. All of these activities will plant the seeds of kindness, which will continue to grow and thrive in their lives as they mature. Kindness won't always be evident immediately, but it will be growing.

Kindness begets kindness, while unkindness multiplies unkindness. Which will you choose to breed, cultivate, and grow?

The kindness children learn within the home will permeate everything they do including friends, school, sports, extra-curricular activities, and most importantly, their digital lives. Kindness in the digital landscape is crucially relevant as children "live" their lives on devices. Ubiquitous screen use has created media-hungry and selfie-centered hearts and minds that too often forget about kindness.

Therefore, as parents we must emphasize and teach digital kindness as much as we do in-person kindness.

How can digital communication be used to reinforce the lesson of kindness? Similarly, how can we teach our children to combat unkindness online?

WORDS OF TONGUE VERSUS WORDS OF TYPE

In the Bible, James makes a fierce declaration to the Jewish-turned-Christian believers regarding the source of words — the tongue:

> *The tongue also is a fire, a world of evil among the parts of the body. It corrupts the whole body, sets the whole course of one's life on fire, and is itself set on fire by hell.*

> James 3:6

Satan has cleverly deceived us to believe there is a difference between *words of the tongue* and *words of type*. More specifically, that our typed words are less potent than our spoken words. A sly move on our enemy's part, but ultimately, we own our words regardless of how they are delivered. Wisdom leads us to understand: just because the word of God doesn't warn against our thumbs being a world of evil among parts of the body, it doesn't mean the words typed on a screen hold less value to God.

We can all acknowledge the greater ease with which typed words flow over their spoken counterparts. One primary reason is the prolific use of screens in our lives. So many tasks such as homework help (just Google it), grocery shopping (order online with home delivery), appointment making (haircuts, doctors), and even ringing a doorbell (text me when you're here) do not require face-to-face or voice-to-voice communication anymore. Additionally, a majority of our children's relationships (and ours, if we are honest) are occurring through screens. Communication is still a priority for us, but it is now primarily via texting, DMs (Direct Messages), Facebook Messenger, Snapchat, and email.

Consequently, our rapid adaptation has left non-verbal cues in its dust. Unkind words spoken face-to-face provides the speaker with immediate emotional reaction and connection. When unkind words are typed, no instant feedback is provided, and interpretation is left to chance. Without feedback and connection, digital words can infect relationships.

This allows unkind digital communication to spread like a virus. It is no coincidence that the Internet uses the term *viral* when referring to the speed and sometimes destructive ways information and words are spread. Unkind digital communication contaminates subtly, slowly shifting everyone's acceptable boundaries further into inappropriateness and even hate. For many, living with unkind digital communication is a part of life. For others, this virus is fatal.

WORDS HAVE THE POWER OF LIFE AND DEATH. SPOKEN OR WRITTEN, EVERYONE MUST OWN THEM AND TAKE RESPONSIBILITY FOR THEIR IMPACT.

Consider the subtle ease with which written words embolden children. An adolescent boy would rarely be brave enough to ask a thirteen-year-old girl to take her clothes off in front of him. However, asking the same girl to text nude pictures is much easier, especially since the boundary line for this type of digital communication has shifted. Similarly, when a young girl comments on a guy's Instagram selfie, "you are fine af [as f**k] — I'd do anything you ask," there is a strong chance she would run and hide if the guy came face-to-face to hold her accountable. Likewise, texting someone "you are better off dead, go kill yourself" becomes easy when you aren't looking that person in the eye.

And parents, we don't get a free pass on this one. While kids text and comment their own cruel and unkind things, we can look no further than news articles, political pieces, and social media profiles to find adults "speaking" similar unkind words. Sometimes these are even more hateful than the cyberbullies our children face.

These digital words leak from our lips and flow through our fingertips. Words have the power of life and death. Spoken or written, everyone must own them and take responsibility for their impact.

TEACHING THROUGH TEXTING

Words flow fast and loose from our children's fingertips while texting. Hundreds per day, thousands per week: these texts document the nature of our children's relationships with their peers, every word revealing their character.

This is the fertile ground where either kindness can grow or unkindness can spread. Parents can use this soil to teach and expect kindness. How will a child know whether the words they are texting are unkind (or considering our last chapter, disrespectful)? They may not receive feedback from the receiver, therefore their feedback must come from us.

Think of it like this: if texting is a sport, you are the head coach. A coach watches his athlete's performance and provides feedback on how to become better. Six-year-olds on a soccer field need a lot of hands-on coaching. They have to learn the fundamentals of the game: the rules, dribbling, passing, and scoring. A coach cannot provide a list of drills, leave for a while, then come back expecting them to have developed elite soccer skills. They need a coach by their side, teaching skills, correcting their errors, and encouraging their success.

On the other hand, a seventeen year old soccer player, who has been coached for many years, doesn't need as much supervision during practice. This teen has far surpassed a basic understanding of the game. Now, he is focused on a strategy to win and perform his personal best. Although the coach knows the teen athlete will perform all the skills taught and honed over the years during a game, he still remains present on the sidelines. Here the coach can observe the entire playing field, his players, and the other team while looking for nuances each athlete cannot see because they are in the middle of it all. When the coach sees an opportunity to adjust the strategy, create a new play, or correct a shortcoming, he calls the athlete to the sidelines, gives a brief talk/reprimand/insight, and then sends him back to the field. With both age groups in our analogy, the coach is always essential. No athlete masters a sport without a coach. Even professional and Olympic athletes have coaches.

The standard to grow kindness is: ***Read what they type; Coach what they say.*** Reading your child's text messages allows you to teach them the fundamentals of texting with respect and kindness. You can coach them through the great and not-so-great plays and provide feedback. Your role will shift from hands-on teaching to sideline observation as they mature. Whether you volunteered for this coaching job or not — it's yours, and no one is coming to replace you. You might as well own it and be the best coach you can be.

Texting will most likely be your child's first method of digital communication, through a device of their own or one shared by the family. As soon as they begin their digital communication, your responsibility as their kindness head coach must begin. Holding your child accountable in their private digital conversations is essential for kindness to grow. We have gone too long assuming children naturally know how to kindly communicate this way. Now we are dealing with painful levels of unkindness. Cyberbullying, shaming, suicides, and hate are spreading among children because they have zero accountability with their digital communication.

This accountability is not an invasion of privacy or an immoral method of parenting. Consider that both the bully and the bullied have a parent or caring adult providing the phone or device. Unkindness can be recognized and stopped by either parent on either side of the texts. Therefore, it is every parent's responsibility to keep their child accountable for their words and to help protect them from the words of others. With this standard, *Read what they type; Coach what they say*, you can promote the growth of kindness, bettering their generation through their circle of influence and creating a lifelong impact on your child's character.

> CYBERBULLYING, SHAMING, SUICIDES, AND HATE ARE SPREADING AMONG CHILDREN BECAUSE THEY HAVE ZERO ACCOUNTABILITY WITH THEIR DIGITAL COMMUNICATION.

If you are thinking, 'I never volunteered to be my child's soccer coach because I don't know (1) the rules of soccer or (2) how to coach' — relax. As long as you understand kindness, you qualify as a coach. The first step is simply reading the texts and evaluating them for kindness.

Are the words they type kind? Are their responses gentle and humble, knowing nonverbal cues and tone of voice are missing? Are they encouraging to others? Are they moral? Are they standing up for what is right and for what the rules are? Do they complement and build others up? Are they texting how they talk? Is their language appropriate?

Or, in contrast, are the words they type cruel and curt? Are they gossiping about others? Shaming others? Are they forwarding junk messages and spam? Do they belittle others or brag about themselves? Do their words feel like bullying? Are they cheating on homework? Are they involved with troublemakers or breaking rules? Do they use language they would never say out loud or to another's face? Are they engaging in sexual talk or sexting? Are they sending racial or offensive memes?

Hopefully, your child's first text messages won't go anywhere near the latter list. Though I assure you, they eventually will.

Provide feedback for your child through routine, calm, face-to-face-conversations. Try your absolute best to be non-confrontational in order to keep communication open. And if their text messages are knocking it out of the kindness park, commend them.

Let's consider how these conversations may play out.

You find a heated text conversation between your son and a friend. You cannot decipher why, but painful words are shared back and forth.

Ask him, "How do you think what you said could be misinterpreted?" Invite him to give you alternative interpretations someone might make. Then provide an example of how his words could have been reworded to avoid a misunderstanding. Ask him additional questions: "Should you have taken more time before deciding what to reply? Was more explanation needed to better your friend's understanding? What would be a kinder way to write this?"

At first, be prepared for zero response from your child. You are coaching a sport he has never played. Allow plenty of time for him to think and respond. Offer ideas and suggestions as necessary. Your job is to stay calm and kind. Your child will absorb what you are teaching, though it may not seem that way at first.

You read a text on your daughter's phone in which a friend calls your daughter a slur of awful names.

Ask your daughter if everything is going okay with her friend. "I noticed she appeared to be pretty upset with you." Listen for clues to understand how being called names made her feel. If your daughter shares the whole story, bring it around to the unkind name calling she received. "Do you think she would have called you those names to your face?" Ask if those words changed the way she feels about the friend, or if she can imagine being angry enough to send similar texts. Seek to bring the realization that it is not okay to send texts like that. Finally, attempt to bring your daughter to a place of forgiveness and reconciliation with her friend. "Based on what we know about her, can you think of a reason why she would have texted you the way she did?" (For example: Are her parents divorcing? Did her boyfriend dump her? Did she fail a test, or get cut from the dance team?)

This type of "girl drama" is common. The best results occur when you catch the drama early enough to coach your daughter how to respond and engage with kindness instead of hurt and anger.

A quick glance over your son's text contacts reveals a new girl interest. The text thread contains sexual references, which based on the girl's response, makes her feel uncomfortable.

It doesn't take very much courage to type bold and persuasive words. Ask your son, "Would you have said those exact words looking this young woman in the eye?" Chances are slim. Discuss what her parents will think of him if or when they read her texts. Play out how this might have made her feel. "Does she feel valued by you or like an object? Does she feel respected?" Our sons need to be coached very specifically in this area because the culture leads them astray. Whether coached by mom or dad, explain that although a woman wants to look outwardly attractive, her heart desires to be internally valued. Ask him, "What could you text a girl to show her you are interested in getting to know her (not just look at and fantasize about her)?" Ultimately, teach him that if he cannot look into the eyes of the girl, her parents, or you and speak the same words — they should never be typed.

These are some of the hardest and most awkward conversations. Be brave, do the hard work, and his character will be better for it.

A quick scan of your high school daughter's texts exposes a wildly inappropriate racial joke.

Ask your daughter to read the text aloud to you. Ask her, "How could these words come back to haunt you?" Encourage her to consider a few scenarios in which her text is shared with others, maybe even virally. What would it look like if she were held accountable for her words? To whom could she be accountable? The individual or group she insulted? The school? The law? God? Because children so rarely visualize any repercussions from what they text, this is an essential exercise! Discuss how she wants to be known by others and if this text would change that. Ask, "Are these the exact words by which you want people judging your character? Would you feel comfortable with other parents, teachers, or coaches reading this? Does this demonstrate arrogance, superiority, or judgment? What about this joke shows kindness to anyone?"

In addition to kindness, our children's written communication should embody every characteristic discussed in this book: Patience, Respect,

Honesty, Self-Control, Humility/Modesty, and Self-Worth.
Kindness is of great importance as it falls away easily with screen to
screen communication, but one character virtue isn't more valuable
than another. Reading and coaching through texts allows
opportunities to teach all these character values to your children.

Ultimately, our emphasis in teaching kindness is to demonstrate how
the virtue changes hearts, moods, and relationships. Our role
modeling and integrity is essential throughout this process. You must
maintain confidentiality within your role as coach. You will read a lot
of their private conversations, and unless they are unkind or truly
need to be addressed, you must remain silent. Not every concern
needs to be addressed; kids should learn resilience in relationships on
their own. Yes, this can be challenging, but our goal isn't to hover
and control — it's to coach for kindness. And yes, coaching can take
a significant amount of time, but all elite athletes are a result of the
coaches who have invested in them. Coach for kindness and watch
elite character develop.

BULLYING AND SHAMING

The prevalence of harsh written words shared over electronic
technology has led to an entirely new struggle for our children:
cyberbullying. According to stopbullying.gov, behavior considered
"bullying" includes the following:

- An Imbalance of Power: Kids who bully use their power —
  such as physical strength, access to embarrassing
  information, or popularity — to control or harm others.
  Power imbalances can change over time and in different
  situations, even if they involve the same people.
- Repetition: Bullying behaviors happen more than once or
  have the potential to happen more than once.[38]

Unfortunately, this "imbalance of power" has met its match with the unlimited power resting in the hands of anyone with an unrestricted device. For better or worse, the Internet and social media now represent equal access to power for everyone. Because access and misuse of this near limitless power has become so ubiquitous, it is of equal importance to include online shaming in this discussion. Shaming involves the publication of private information on the Internet. Generally speaking, the sole purpose of online shaming is to publicly humiliate a person.[39]

Recall how subtly and silently the unkind digital communication virus spreads. Bullying and shaming creeps into our children's lives the same way. Often children hide the signs and symptoms as the virus infects them. Fear keeps them bound in further silence.

This is where the unkind virus turns into a deadly infection.

- In 2007, thirteen-year-old Megan Meier hanged herself after her boyfriend, Josh, whom she met over Myspace, broke up with her and told her, "The world is better without you." It turns out Josh was fictitious, a fake account a former friend and her mom created for the sole purpose of shaming and bulling Megan.[40]

- In 2008, eighteen-year-old Jessica Logan hanged herself after a nude picture she sent to her boyfriend ended up being massively distributed across her city and through social media platforms.[41]
- In 2010, Tyler Clenti jumped off the George Washington Bridge to his death after his freshman college roommate used a webcam to broadcast footage of him kissing another man in their dorm room.[42]

- In 2012, sixteen-year-old Amanda Todd took her life after years of being stalked and shamed. After exposing her breasts over an online video chat in seventh grade, the recipient blackmailed her with the picture and spread it virally. Amanda created a YouTube video and through the use of note cards publicly shared her struggle with online shaming. One month later, she took her own life.[43]

- In 2014, eighteen-year-old Conrad Roy III was found dead of carbon monoxide poisoning in his pick-up truck. His seventeen-year-old girlfriend, Michelle Carter, sent him a barrage of text messages encouraging him to go through with it and even to get back into the truck when he had second thoughts. In 2017, Michelle Carter was convicted of involuntary manslaughter in a landmark trial, holding her accountable for the text messages and knowledge of her boyfriend's suicide. In court it was stated that Michelle's text went from "words of kindness and love to aggressively encouraging him to carry out his suicide threats."[44]

- In 2017, eleven-year-old Tysen Benz hanged himself within two hours of receiving messages through text and Snapchat that his thirteen-year-old girlfriend was dead. Tysen, unaware it was a prank, replied over social media that he, too, was going to kill himself. No one involved told an adult or Tysen that it was all a prank. After 3 weeks on life support, Tysen passed away.[45]

These are only a *few* cases detailing the horror of bullying, shaming, and the immense power of careless words. Countless more stories involving depression, cutting, self-harm, and suicide exist that are never talked about in mainstream media. Non-suicidal self-harm is on the rise among adolescents.[46] Among adolescent girls specifically, severe depression rose by 58 percent and the suicide rate increased 65 percent over five years from 2010-2015.[47] There are certainly questions about the correlation to the rise of digital communication and cyberbullying. However, it is important to acknowledge that phones, the Internet, and social media are simply tools used to bully and shame. Behind the screen is always a person. We cannot control every person on the Internet, but we can control who has access to our children and who and what our children have access to.

Bullying may seem like a problem with no solutions, but we are worse off if we throw our hands up in apathetic consent instead of educating ourselves. With knowledge, we can act intentionally to transform our culture's attitudes toward unkind online communication, one child at a time.

There are three prominent areas in which bullying and shaming begin.

Pictures

We can prevent our children's shattered innocence by prohibiting the deadly cocktail of cameras, video, and online access. When it comes to cyberbullying and digital harassment, an embarrassing picture or video is all someone needs as ammunition; therefore, don't be afraid to turn off the camera on your child's phone. Blocking the ability for your children to send or receive pictures can also curb the spread of this unkindness. These precautions are neither cruel nor child abuse! It is simply acknowledging that children are growing up in a culture with access to unlimited power.

A popular form of communication among children today are apps that allow or enable vanishing pictures. Instagram and Snapchat, among others, provide users the ability to send pictures that "disappear" once the recipient has viewed them for a length of time as determined by the sender. This deceives kids into believing it is safe to send inappropriate content. Any picture or written material that appears for a short time only to disappear "forever" can still render devastating consequences. These vanishing functionalities cannot be easily monitored by parents; therefore, if you do nothing else to prevent bullying and shaming, block apps that allow for sending and receiving of vanishing pictures.

Messaging and Anonymous Apps

If children want to privatize their digital communication, they usually turn to one of the popular messaging apps such as Kik or WhatsApp. These apps are commonly used on devices functioning solely on WiFi, without any cellular service plan. These apps have been implicated in numerous bullying, sexting, and trafficking cases because of the ease in connecting with anyone.[48] In general, these apps are internet based, allow for anonymous profiles without age verification, and allow conversations within to be hidden or deleted. While there are some programs that can recover deleted threads through messaging apps, there remains no healthy reason to use these over standard text messages, which are stored on the phone. For program details visit: https://managingmediabook.com/resources

Similarly, if a child has something to say yet desires to remain hidden, anonymous apps allow users to publicly post anything without identifying themselves. Several of these apps have come and gone, but a few successful apps are: Whisper, Afterschool, and tbh (To Be Honest). These apps are wildly popular and utilize either geographically defined areas, schools' names, or your personal contacts from your device to generate an audience. Most of these apps claim to promote a community of encouragement and fun, but the freedom anonymity gives doesn't tend to bring out the best side in teens. Rumor spreading, shaming, and bullying are entirely too easy on these apps, but all of this can be prevented when access is restricted.

A hard and fast rule as kids begin using a device or phone is: if you cannot monitor activity within an app, your children should not be allowed to use it.

Social Media

It is frustrating that something with the potential to be good and helpful can be equally used to hate, bully, and shame. Within social media apps, anyone with an opinion can speak his or her unkindness through comments, private messages, and posting of pictures. All of which can be made public. Too often teens believe that when something is posted and deleted, it is gone for good. Not at all! Social media companies may keep records of everything, not to mention screen shots which can be taken and shared. Furthermore, people rarely conceptualize how big a problem this will be in the future as technology is developed to aggregate every piece of online information on someone. From facial recognition to high-powered algorithms, we are nearly to the day when no one will be able to hide from their online history.

So is the answer to keep your kids off social media completely? Yes, at least while they are young, impulsive, and immature. Aside from the addictive nature of social media, its public nature along with the ramped escalation of unkindness, bullying, and shaming should be enough reason to delay exposure to these platforms. But if that isn't convincing enough, research has also shown the reward pathway of 'likes' mimics that of heroin inside the brain.[49]

Yet I know many of you have already allowed or in the future will allow social media accounts. At a certain age it can be wise to teach them how to use popular social media accounts appropriately. I recommend sixteen years old, but will discuss this more in Chapter 7. Kindness rules apply on social media, as they do with texting. Create the account with your child — you alone know the password — and

monitor it regularly. Know and follow your child's activity closely to ensure kindness is evident. Discuss what type of content they post or comment on. Ask how their words, whether in a post or a comment, reflect their character.

Be vigilant and persistent regarding who they are allowed to follow or friend and who are following or friending them. Allow for one degree of separation when accepting friends/followers. One degree means someone they have had a face-to-face conversation with — someone in their school, church, or sports team. This is not your friend's cousin's coworker's boss who was suggested by Instagram. There is no reason to allow relatively unknown strangers to have open and unlimited access to your child. Additionally, block any followers or friends who are unkind or display a tendency to bully or shame others. Operate with a zero tolerance for bullying, shaming, and unkindness. Do not be afraid to pull the social media plug completely if there is any bullying or shaming occurring.

This topic is of growing concern among parents, teachers, administrators, and policy makers as news headlines permeate our consciousness with tragic story after tragic story. The sad truth is the online and often anonymous nature of bullying and shaming makes it more common and difficult to avoid. The culture of narcissism and "selfie-ness" has fueled this already burning fire with self-promotion, competition, and jealousy. Kindness is the only extinguisher for this raging fire. Like an old-time water brigade, buckets of kindness passed from one person to the next unite the people in purpose and smother the smoldering embers of hate and discord. When kindness is shared online, it possesses the power of an opened hydrant. The flow of kindness drowns out negativity with its positive force.

Kindness is the answer.

TO THE NAYSAYERS

The virulent lie of 'children deserve complete privacy online and on phones' is contaminating parents everywhere. Some rigidly believe, above all else, that a child needs to know their parents trust them; therefore, they reason, reading their texts or monitoring their social media would demonstrate a lack of trust.

While it is true that a child does have a core need to feel trusted, this has little to do with privacy. Trusting your child to be kind will be easy. Trusting everyone else they connect or have contact with, on the other hand, should make you uncomfortable. Ultimately, if a child truly valued privacy, he or she wouldn't share the entire spectrum of life's activities over the infinitely public Internet. In fact, most teens these days consider privacy to be a thing of the past — public platform is their normal. The only privacy children desire is from anyone who holds them accountable. Namely: parents. They want to post or say anything and not be held accountable for the consequences of their choices.

> IF A CHILD TRULY VALUED PRIVACY, HE OR SHE WOULDN'T SHARE THE ENTIRE SPECTRUM OF LIFE'S ACTIVITIES OVER THE INFINITELY PUBLIC INTERNET.

Consider also the features built into social media platforms that allow the blocking and unfollowing of certain 'friends' — often without the other's knowledge. Social media engineers want kids to have the ability to say and do anything without the accountability of Mom, Dad, or Grandma. Otherwise, kids won't ritualistically come back and share their precious data with the platform.

In the end, it isn't about deserving privacy, but rather deserving confidentiality.

We can check their text messages, emails, social media profiles, and comments they've made to ensure kindness and safety while vowing all non-life-threatening information we see is confidential. This means you don't mention that new girl your son is talking to at the dinner table or criticize your daughter's study habits because you read a text describing how she didn't get her homework done.

The heart behind monitoring their digital communication isn't snooping: it is safety. Nor should our hearts yearn to catch them in something, but rather to teach kindness in everything. Unlike a high school football coach who may scream and shame in front of an entire team, our coaching is done privately and in love.

The best thing any parent can do is get involved and engage in their children's lives. Genuinely care about their heart and how they treat others. Train their thoughts to be kind, and kindness will eventually overflow into their spoken and written words. Begin continual conversations about kindness and its importance. Acknowledge and compliment your child's kind acts or those of others around you. Value kindness every day, and it will grow.

If you teach and coach effective and kind digital communication early on, many of these monitors will not be necessary as they move up into high school. For the first-time "texter" or smartphone user, particularly those in elementary or middle school, monitoring should be non-negotiable.

Read what they type; Coach what they say.

Kindness has no regrets.

BIBLICAL BACKING FOR KINDNESS

The book of Proverbs provides a wealth of resources to encourage our children's choice of words, both spoken and written. These are NLT version, easily understood by children:

A fool's proud talk becomes a rod that beats him, but the words of the wise keep them safe. (14:3)

A gentle answer deflects anger, but harsh words make tempers flare. (15:1)

Gentle words are a tree of life; a deceitful tongue crushes the spirit. (15:4)

A hot-tempered person starts fights; a cool-tempered person stops them. (15:18)

Everyone enjoys a fitting reply; it is wonderful to say the right thing at the right time! (15:23)

The heart of the godly thinks carefully before speaking; the mouth of the wicked overflows with evil words. (15:28)

From a wise mind comes wise speech; the words of the wise are persuasive. (16:23)

Kind words are like honey — sweet to the soul and healthy for the body. (16:24)

A truly wise person uses few words; a person with understanding is even-tempered. (17:27)

Fools have no interest in understanding; they only want to air their own opinions. (18:2)

The mouths of fools are their ruin; they trap themselves with their lips. (18:7)

Rumors are dainty morsels that sink deep into one's heart. (18:8)

Spouting off before listening to the facts is both shameful and foolish. (18:13)

The human spirit can endure a sick body, but who can bear a crushed spirit? (18:14)

There are "friends" who destroy each other, but a real friend sticks closer than a brother. (18:24)

A gossip goes around telling secrets, so don't hang around with chatterers. (20:19)

Watch your tongue and keep your mouth shut, and you will stay out of trouble. (21:23)

Direct your children onto the right path, and when they are older, they will not leave it. (22:6)

CHAPTER FOUR

Honesty:
No lies, nothing deleted

*Honesty is more than not lying. It is truth
telling, truth speaking, truth living, and
truth loving.*[50]

James E. Faust

My two oldest children are girls, almost five years apart. They are not
biologically related, but they share the bond of adoption, estrogen,
and frustration with our phone and media rules.

They both wanted phones so desperately that asking them to practice
patience brought on tears. They desired what every other teen, tween,
and sadly many elementary school students in our upper-middle class
suburb have: a smartphone. But instead, they were stuck with parents
who didn't watch television, Netflix, or R-rated movies and who care
more about their character than their desire for a phone. You can
imagine how their annoyance with us strengthened their bond.

Ryan and I planned to buy a phone for our oldest over the summer of 2013, but we held out till the very last moment before school started, for no other reason than we were dreading the purchase. We knew one thing for certain: how we handled the first phone would set the standard for every other phone entering our home. We had pre-committed to a handful of rules, one of them being no social media accounts. I knew enough about social media to convince me that it wasn't in the best interest for a newly adopted teenager who had spent nine years in poverty and around drugs, then six years in the foster care system.

As one can imagine, that commitment went over as smoothly as 40-grit sandpaper, overshadowing any excitement she felt to simply have her own smartphone. She constantly grumbled about the phone's uselessness without social media. She described how she "needed" Facebook to connect with old friends, "needed" Instagram to edit photos, "needed" Twitter to follow Justin Bieber, and "needed" Snapchat to communicate with current friends. She was a teenager, and because social media is where teenagers live, she wanted to live in that world too. Social media, she foolishly claimed, was the only thing that would motivate her to study and work hard.

But we wouldn't allow it.

We knew better. She may have been our first teenager, but we had enough technological, psychological, and biblical knowledge to know this was Satan's deception. For her, social media would function only as smoke and mirrors. It would provide her with a false reality to become whoever she wanted to be behind her screen. We also knew it would open up access for connections to be made with people from her traumatic past, potentially to her detriment. Based on what we knew about social media leading to anxiety and depression, we could not in clear conscience place such a large stumbling block in front of her.

We held our ground while she fought back for months. Finally, it seemed she had surrendered to our rigid stance. Little did we know, however, she had simply surrendered to not getting what she wanted from *us*. Behind the scenes, she had bypassed our "tremendously unfair" rules. She was unable to pass her high school academic classes, but she had incredible circumvention skills. She had a deep desire to find worth and validation, and thus craved social media attention like it was her next "fix." Starving for soul-satisfying self-worth, she opted for the quick fixes of social media sugar. Dishonesty was a necessary step to obtain what she wanted. Using her friends' old and discarded phones and even our home computer, she managed a fix every day.

We didn't know any of this, until her younger sister spoke up. With a subtle mention of her sister's "Facebook boyfriend," the scales fell from our eyes, and we knew that somehow, someway, our oldest was fooling us. In hindsight, we should have known the moment she stopped complaining and accepted our rules that something wasn't right. Sometimes though, it just feels so good not to struggle every day. These are moments when the "best parent ever" feeling pushes us into complacency. Fortunately, we had installed a monitoring program on our family PC, which enabled us to verify what we heard. No matter how many lies our oldest told to cover up her deception, this program exposed the truth. What we discovered went far beyond a teen's desire to connect with old friends. We found cyber relationships initiated and maintained in an attempt to traffic our daughter. There were numerous vicious fights through social media platforms with other girls over a boy (including death threats). We read about potential illegal acts with horrific language throughout. She had also established a multitude of profiles where she pretended to be someone different in each one.

As we worked through the discipline and correction of our oldest daughter, we also attempted damage control with our accidental whistle-blower. Ultimately, she didn't want to feel like a snitch or lose her sister's trust. And in her defense, her admission about the Facebook boyfriend was completely absent of malice or ill-intent. My husband and I talked to her about the importance, yet difference, between keeping a secret and keeping someone safe. We really hoped she would see her admission as lifesaving instead of snitching. In the end, we reinforced the old but true maxim: honesty is always the best policy.

Two years later, this same younger daughter had the opportunity to demonstrate what she had learned about honesty. As she enjoyed her summer freedom before the beginning of eighth grade, she also delighted in her first iPhone. Like her older sister, she disliked our rules and routinely begged to have social media. Again, we did not relent. We were keenly aware of her ability to use someone else's phone or device to gain access, but we hoped she'd learned enough from her sister's mistakes. We checked her phone regularly, but due to the limited access we impose for the first year of smartphone ownership, we found very little that needed coaching or correction.

Late one evening that summer, she appeared at our bedroom door emotionally overcome and clearly needing to confess something. We invited her in and sat focused as she disclosed her recent behavior. Through sobs, she bravely admitted, "I found Snapchat in our iCloud, downloaded it, used it, and then deleted it each day, so you wouldn't know."

Immediately, my husband and I recalled how we downloaded Snapchat to try it out and see what all the hype was about. We knew it was in our iCloud, but we thought we had restricted her ability to download from the cloud without a password. Clearly, we hadn't. We asked her, "How long has this been going on?"

"About two weeks. I knew you would eventually find out, and I wanted to be honest and upfront before you did." She regretted her transgression and felt convicted to come clean.

I cannot deny that we were frustrated — partially at ourselves. At the same time, however, her honesty and willingness to come forward and courageously speak the truth was supremely significant in our eyes. She was right; we would have found out. And, yes, if we had found out before she confessed, her punishment would have been worse than it actually was.

She understood and respected that honesty is the best policy. She may have been carried adrift by her desire to have social media, but her anchor was honesty.

THE BEST POLICY, THE HARDEST VIRTUE

The cliché "honesty is the best policy" is often viewed as an unwise and outdated proverb. We live in a culture in which loose lips and untamed tongues appear to garner fame and success. Every day it seems we learn of a public figure or popular icon using dishonesty to his or her advantage. Interestingly, while dishonest behavior may grant them immediate gratification or even elevate their careers for a time, the exposed truth all but destroys them. Athletes like Lance Armstrong and Tiger Woods, entrepreneur Martha Stewart, stock broker Bernard Madoff, American Presidents Richard Nixon and Bill Clinton, movie producer Harvey Weinstein, and television news reporters Brian Williams and Matt Lauer all learned the importance of honesty and character.

Currently, we have a new societal obsession with and reliance on news as entertainment. This has incited a fierce competition between network TV/radio broadcasts and Internet news sites, pushing the boundary of truth increasingly farther from reality. A survey published by Pew Research in August 2017 found that 67 percent of Americans get their news through social media[51] while an online poll revealed only 23 percent felt very confident that they could tell real news from fake news.[52]

Confusion, it seems, is a common side effect to this new level of global connectedness which grants us access to more media, more information, and, sadly, more lies.

We cannot attribute all the blame to culture. Dishonest behavior has been a sin long displayed throughout the history of mankind. It began with Adam and Even in the garden and continues today all over the Internet, in schools, and in homes. There is absolutely no denying, honesty was — and always will be — hard to maintain.

It is equally hard to teach children to be honest. As the parents and role models, we have the same propensity to be dishonest. Think of the common lies parents tell their kids today: tooth fairies, "you're allergic to soda," or "No! I'm not eating candy, I'm eating broccoli." While these are somewhat funny examples, more severe lies can grow and destroy the parent/child relationship. Many parents (moms especially) have grown accustom to dishonestly posting on social media. Whether to pretend perfection or to illicit attention, inauthenticity is Satan's newest and subtle ploy to make our lies feel socially acceptable.

When it comes to the character God desires, the word of God is clear that honesty is a priority.

My children, come. Listen to me. I will teach you to have respect for the Lord.

Do you love life and want to see many good days?

Then keep your tongues from speaking evil. Keep your
lips from telling lies.

Turn away from evil, and do good. Look for peace,
and go after it.

Psalm 34:11-14 (NIRV)

The Psalmist sought to teach children the reward of pursuing the character God desires. He makes it clear that respect, kindness, and honesty are not only highly valued but also blessed. To train and equip new believers in Jesus Christ on how to act as Christians, the Apostle Peter went on to recite those words (1 Peter 3:10-12). Peter encourages the believers to continue exemplifying respect, kindness, and honesty even when it causes suffering. Still true today, choosing honesty over lies or omissions can lead to temporary suffering. This is what makes the virtue hard, but read Peter's answer to the question he knew we would all ask: "Why would I choose to suffer?"

But even if you should suffer for what is right, you are
blessed. Do not fear their threats; do not be frightened.

1 Peter 3:14

What do these instructions — *keep your tongues from speaking evil and your lips from telling lies* — look like in the context of parenting your child in the digital age? Let's start at the foundation.

Honesty should be a foundational principle and commitment you honor in all aspects of your family. It means you bless honesty even when honesty leads to discipline or correction. Why? Because honesty is hard and takes practice. In these scenarios, we are able to disciple our children, showing them Jesus's love and forgiveness.

94

Jesus forgives our wrongs and remembers them no more when we come before him with honest confession and repentance. Are there consequences or repercussions for our wrongdoings? Yes, but we receive the blessing of forgiveness. The same is true for our children. Therefore, we forgive and bless honest confessions from our children. Consequences may still occur, but honesty is blessed.

IT'S A MATTER OF BECOMING A FAMILY WHO TELLS THE TRUTH, LOVES THE TRUTH, AND LIVES THE TRUTH.

We can bless our children and honor their honesty through positively affirming their character and explaining how their honesty builds trust. Nonetheless, lessons are learned and poor choices are avoided as a result of consequences. Therefore, there must be an equal balance of both blessings and consequences. In the situation with my daughter and Snapchat, she incurred an immediate and appropriate consequence for her actions while at the same time praise and validation for her choice to be honest. Later, I was able to say to her, "Because you have shown honesty and integrity in the past, I trust you with this new responsibility. If something goes awry, I know you will be honest with me." She learned not to sneak apps and earned trust at the same time.

It's a matter of becoming a family who tells the truth, loves the truth, and lives the truth. Every one of us will make mistakes and tell lies, but when truth and honesty are the foundation, our character will be one which God desires.

THE REALITIES OF SCREENS

A *screen*, by one definition, is *anything which conceals*.[53] This is consistent with how our digital screens can effectively *conceal* our lies (the ability to delete content and conversations), *conceal* our identity (anonymous sharing apps and fake accounts), and *conceal* our sin (apps like Snapchat where inappropriate pictures are automatically deleted).

Concealed or not, every spoken or written lie or exaggeration creates an alternate reality in which the liar must live. Each faux reality must be maintained — lest the truth be exposed. Imagine trying to navigate through hormones, increasing responsibilities, academics, and relationships as a tween or teen all while living in multiple, digital realities built on lies. This can place unimaginable pressure on children.

The downward spiral our children find themselves in is their reliance on the screen. They love their screens and desire to connect to everyone, but it is the screen itself that provides fertile soil to plant and grow lies. In other words, it feels good, but it also gets them into trouble. More online connections can equal the potential for more lies, more exaggerations, more deceit, and more realities to be maintained. All of which requires more time on the screen. The lack of stability in this downward spiral drives them right back to the screen for another soothing hit of the pleasure chemical dopamine, in the form of a new text, snap, like, comment, or follower. And the downward slide continues.

Here's the deal, though: Truth telling requires connection and relationship. It follows verbal communication, eye contact, and, often, appropriate physical touch. Honesty requires vulnerability with another person. All of these are completely absent with online and screen-based communication and connection. Therefore, screen based communication makes both honesty and relationships hard. As seen with adults on social media, inauthenticity is most often the result.

When relationships are difficult and lack authenticity, emotional health begins to suffer. The downward spiral of screens can land our children in a pit of depression, anxiety, and addiction.

Parents, we have the responsibility to keep our children from the downward spiral of this screen cycle. If psychologists believe our teenagers are on the verge of a mental health crisis, we would be wise to do everything we can to keep our children from spiraling down to those depths.

It's time to elevate honesty. Lies separate us from God while honesty draws us closer in our relationship with Him. The enemy wants to widen the divide by devaluing honest character. We cannot give him an inch of ground in our children's lives.

ACCOUNTABILITY

Until our children have matured and grown to regard honesty as their foundation, we must teach and protect them through accountability. A basic precedent for accountability is this: If you type it, capture it, play it, download it, or send it, you are allowing me to see it.

If you pay for your child's device or phone, along with their service plan, and they are under eighteen years old, you have every right to see anything on the phone. As we discussed in the previous chapter, your role is to coach them, and that only happens when the content is visible, not hidden or deleted. In the course of life, a time will come when you begin to withdraw your accountability as they prepare for life after high school. Until then, it is your responsibility to hold them accountable for their activity — most especially, their dishonest activity.

The standard to hold children accountable to the character virtue of honesty is: *No lies, nothing deleted*.

One of the most fertile grounds for dishonesty is text messages. They flow fast and furious, often between multiple people at a time. Emotion, sincerity, and humor are often measured only through the emojis added.

Often, children gain experience texting before they have their own smartphone. With accountability, texting can provide a safe and effective start to digital communication. Using text messaging accountability — *No lies, nothing deleted* — will provide teachable moments for building honest communication habits that can be maintained as they mature.

> IF YOU ARE WILLING TO TYPE IT, CAPTURE IT, PLAY IT, DOWNLOAD IT, OR SEND IT, YOU ARE ALLOWING MOM & DAD TO SEE IT.

Although digital communication is now commonplace for adults, it is still a privilege for children who are learning the basics tenants of verbal and written communication. Children are bound to make mistakes when learning digital communication, which is why we must watch and teach through these moments. But often, lies through texting are blatant — not accidental. Cunning children also learn to delete inappropriate text messages in an effort to hide their lies or wrongdoings. When a child first receives a phone with text message capabilities or text messaging through a home smartphone, explain the basic tenets for the text messaging privilege:

1. We will be able to see deleted messages, so don't try to hide anything. For program recommendations to view and recover deleted text messages, visit: https://managingmediabook.com/resources

2. No swearing, bullying, shaming, or arguments of any kind allowed over texts.

3. No lying, embellishing, or self-aggrandizing in order to impress people.

4. You are responsible for gently correcting anyone who texts inappropriate messages to you. If you do not, we will block them. Most Cellular services providers offer parental limits for a small monthly fee, allowing parents to block or "blacklist" unwanted contacts.

These expectations build habits of honest digital communication. Imagine if parents had been teaching this standard for the past ten years. Would bullying be as prevalent if parents held their children accountable for the words they texted? Would the suicide rate among adolescent girls be up 200 percent[54] if online shamers were held accountable by their parents? I believe we would see greater character in people today if *No lies, nothing deleted* had been the standard from the beginning of SMS. But it's never too late to implement the standard! We can begin now and help reshape our children's generation.

Modifying your child's behavior requires your active participation. Challenge them to be honest, and don't settle for dishonest character because you don't have time to keep them accountable. You have to make time. It is entirely too important not to and it is your responsibility.

Accountability can also mean discipline. In our parental fantasy land, we only have to tell our children once, and they listen and obey. In reality, however, it often takes multiple warnings and consequences to teach valuable lessons. If a child is perpetually telling lies or deleting conversations, be brave! Take their phone away, turn off text messaging, or find a creative way to drive the lesson home. No, you won't be their favorite person at that moment, but you must remember: the future dividends of proven character are worth it.

Accountability means we check their phones — reading their texts for truthfulness and looking for deleted or hidden content. We teach our children this standard and give them tools to maintain it, so that when they are older, they will not depart from the truth.

THIS STANDARD AT WORK

Here is how this standard of *No lies, nothing deleted* worked recently in my life.

Back in the introduction of this book, I told the story of the sexually provocative text message thread I'd found from a boy to my daughter. It had gone from zero to one hundred in a matter of days, all the while my husband and I had been lax on routinely checking.

The beauty of this story and of the expectation of honesty is this: When I found the text thread, I found all of it. My daughter had not deleted anything — just as our expectations require. She knew the conversation had crossed a line, but she was paralyzed and too scared to know how to get out. Later, she admitted how she was waiting for us to find the thread, step in, and help her out of it.

We took time to discuss with our daughter where the conversation went wrong. We inquired how the texts made her feel, and we also empowered her with kind but truthful responses she could use if this were to ever happen again. We gave insight to where the boy was coming from (something her innocent and inexperienced brain didn't yet know) and encouraged her to honor and value herself enough to stop or never engage in conversations like this in the first place.

The most important motive with this standard of *No lies, nothing deleted* is to provide an opportunity to coach through these experiences. When they are young and just beginning to communicate behind screens, the first lessons can be the most important. I can almost guarantee every child will participate in dishonest text conversations at some point. Chances are, they will respond poorly and delete the thread – not because they are bad, but because they are inexperienced and have not been taught.

Furthermore, the *No lies* portion of this standard cuts right to the heart of our children's propensity to tell "little white" lies and over exaggerated claims in text messages. It is simply way too easy to lie and exaggerate in texts without eye contact and nonverbal cues to tip off the recipient. If children consistently get away with the lies, lying becomes habit. If you can bring about awareness of them, humility brings them back to honesty. The intent should never to be to embarrass your child. With kindness and gentleness, the lies must be addressed so honesty can be maintained.

HOW TO KEEP THEM HONEST

Everyone wants honest children, and hopefully by now, you are convinced that you need to work hard on accountability to build up your child's ability to maintain honest character. The question I know you are asking is, "How do you uphold this standard?" Perhaps more specifically, "How do you know if they are deleting or hiding texts and content?"

1. **Only use Apple**. They are vastly easier to lock down, keep

secure, and recover information from. Android-based phones can be used, but they require third party apps to maintain safety and security.

2. **Purchase a data recovery program**. This allows retrieval of texts, pictures, contacts, videos, call logs, and more.

3. **Only parents know the password to iTunes or Google Play**. Essentially, this will keep children from having the opportunity to be dishonest. If they can download anything without your permission, they will. Make it easier for them to maintain honesty by removing the temptation. This is one of the best ways to protect them from the dishonest influences around them.

4. **Utilize built-in restrictions (iOS) or third party app-locking services (Android)**. All iPhones have iCloud. When a family has multiple devices through one iTunes account, they gain the ability to share downloaded apps through the cloud. Because not all apps are appropriate for all ages, you have to disable Installing Apps. This removes the temptation to download freely from the cloud. Similarly, you can disable the ability to Delete Apps as a method to keep apps once installed.

For detailed instructions on smartphone parental controls for Apple and Android phones, as well as data recovery programs visit: https://managingmediabook.com/resources

These practical methods for maintaining the honesty standard work extremely well, but the world outside our control has equal access to our children. Children have a plethora of time and determination to find covert ways around our standards. I wish we didn't need the following information, but we cannot be so naïve that we neglect keeping ourselves fully informed.

HOW THEY WILL TRY TO HIDE FROM YOU

Children can engage in a host of other communication methods through screens, including (1) social media apps like Facebook, Snapchat, Instagram, Twitter, and Kik, (2) texting websites such as textnow.com, textplus.com, textem.net, go-text.me, txt2day.com, etc., and (3) the parent's phone or other devices in the home.

Let's explore this a bit more.

Social Media

By allowing social media, you allow communication to take place that you may never see or know about. Social media apps are web-based, and information (posted or received) is not stored on the phone or device itself. Therefore, data recovery programs cannot retrieve deleted threads of messages sent through social media apps like Facebook or Instagram.

One option for accountability is to have the login and password for their accounts and do spot/random checks for honesty. For apps allowing disappearing content (such as Snapchat and Instagram), I must warn you of its propensity to harbor dishonest behavior for one obvious reason: the content disappears. It isn't difficult to imagine a child's temptation to lie, embellish, or self-aggrandize when they believe their lie will last only ten seconds. For this reason, I recommend avoiding these apps.

A second option for accountability is third party monitoring programs such as TeenSafe or OurPact. These web based services connects with your child's social media accounts, receives all their data, and then analyzes it via algorithms to detect issues such as cyberbullying, sexting, drug-related content, and depression. These programs grant the ability to place time limits and restrictions, as well as provides summaries of your child's activity for you. A concern with this option is granting another third party organization access to all of your child's content. If the monitoring program is compromised, all of your child's social media account information may also be compromised.

Texting Websites

Like social media platforms, websites and apps providing free texting do not allow for the retrieval of deleted content. The best way to prevent these from tempting your child is to withhold the iTunes or Google Play password, so they cannot be installed. Apps like Kik, also discussed in the previous chapter, are free texting apps. Kik is designed to maintain anonymity and remain hidden from parents and has been associated with both suicides and murders.[55] If the ability to download such an app is present, temptation and peer pressure can easily overrule honesty.

Another feature available in iOS Restrictions or through third party apps on Android, allows blocking specific websites. Here, you can block the free online texting websites, as well as any other websites you'd prefer your children not have access to.

Devices in Your Home

You must maintain boundaries across all devices in your home — including your own. Kids will look for the easiest way around a limitation. Often it is a parent's phone or device children turn to because it rarely has parental restrictions turned on. Therefore, all parents should have restrictions enabled on their own phones, as well. You will know your own password to bypass the restriction settings should you need to. Most importantly, having your smartphone password protected will prohibit your child from accessing inappropriate content on your device. Think about it: how often do you check your own website history, deleted text threads, and such? Probably never — and children know this! Restrict your own phone and every other device in the home. Remove the temptation and opportunity for dishonesty.

Human nature, especially in adolescents and teenagers, tends to seek opportunities to benefit and satisfy self. If you never give your child an expectation to be honest in all their online activities and never hold them accountable for dishonesty, they will choose what benefits them in the moment. What benefits self in the moment, when compounded with the influence of fickle emotions, peer pressure, popularity, friends, and culture, can be dangerous and have a devastating, lifelong impact.

On the contrary, when honesty is not only modeled but also taught and held in high regard, the question, "What benefits self?" is easily answered with: Being honest before God and with Mom and Dad is best for me.

Choosing not to limit or hold your child accountable for the sake of personal solace, apathy, or ignorance doesn't benefit your child's character. In fact, this choice is more likely to damage their character and future relationships. Honesty is learned through tangible relationships and open communication. Our relationship with our children is the best place to begin their lesson. When they know honesty is expected, they learn to value it.

Recently, I felt the Holy Spirit telling me that one of my children was up to no good. I questioned each of them, but I discovered nothing. After a few days of feeling sick with concern, my husband and I finally downloaded the content on their phones with a data recovery program. We quickly found out exactly what was going on and the source of our foreboding feelings. Yes, there were deleted texts and lies. It was ugly and heart-breaking, but in the end, truth prevailed and beautiful lessons were learned. Because the deleted texts and lies were discovered, we were able to save our child from slipping further into sin and destroying relationships and opportunities. While I'd love for my children to value honesty as much as I do, I know they won't just yet. They are adolescents and teens with still-developing brains and faith. They are learning, though. The more we hold them accountable for honesty, love them, and demonstrate forgiveness, the more they will grow to understand and value truth.

The core characteristics we've covered so far — patience, respect, kindness, and honesty — are like muscles. The more they are worked, the stronger and more resilient they become. This does not mean working these muscles is always fun. It is painful in the moment and often for days afterward. But, oh, how glorious it will be when we and our children have enough strength to move mountains!

CHAPTER FIVE

Self-Control:
Limited time and quantity

Educate your children to self-control, to the habit of holding passion and prejudice and evil tendencies subject to upright and reasoning will, and you will have done much to abolish misery from their future and crimes from society.[56]

Benjamin Franklin

When I adopted one of my daughters, she was fifteen years old. She had lived most of her life in the same large metropolis where I lived.

Claiming its status as the seventh largest city in the United States, San Antonio has every restaurant, store, and venue one could imagine. Our suburb was cut from the same wool as every other developing American city. Within a ten-minute drive is every high-end retail store and the American Mom staples of Target, Costco, Chick-fil-A, and Starbucks.

My daughter, in contrast, did not have access to or the privilege of such luxuries and conveniences. She had resided in low-income housing before she became custody of the state and lived in several different foster homes.

It wasn't that she had never visited any of these stores and businesses; however, her experiences at them differed greatly from those of my already-adopted children. While my six-year-old son knew Target's toy section with photographic-memory precision, my daughter had never shopped there. Her toys were few, and she rarely had the pleasure of selecting her own. Even more so, she didn't attend lunch play dates at Chick-fil-A and never imagined asking for a Starbucks hot chocolate on a cold day. These middle-class norms were not her realities.

About one month into her placement with us, she and I made a quick trip to an office supply store to grab some school supplies. As we finished shopping, I decided to propose an impromptu Starbucks date. We were in the middle of the hard, brave work it takes to form a parent-child bond when fifteen years are lost. I jumped at any chance for the two of us to experience one-on-one time together to strengthen our relationship.

"I have an awesome idea! Let's stop at Starbucks before heading home."

Rather than joy or anticipation lighting up her face, the emotion that flashed in her eyes was apprehension, if not outright fear. When I gently probed, she confessed that she had never been to Starbucks and had no idea if she would like it.

I eased her trepidation and removed all pressure. "If you don't like it, we can just throw it away. You won't have to drink it." *Or I'll drink it, because who would really waste Starbucks like that!?!*

When we approached the young man at the register to place our order, she still hadn't decided what she wanted to try. I told our hipster barista, "This is my daughter's first time at Starbucks, so she's not sure what to order. Do you have any suggestions?"

My statement took him completely aback. "What do you mean you've never been to Starbucks? Where are you from? They don't, like, have Starbucks there, or what?" My daughter's gaze dropped as she tried to laugh off the comment without answering.

I grimaced over his production, and he quickly recovered from his shock and offered suggestions. "You look like you're in high school. All of the high school girls get Frappuccinos. It's, like, the 'chic drink.'"

After agreeing to try the barista's suggestion, she drank her first caramel Frappuccino on that hot, August afternoon. She was a changed girl.

What "Drinking the Kool-Aid" was to Generation X is now "Drinking the Frappuccino" to young Millennials and iGen. Once you've tasted one, you're hooked, and Starbucks becomes a lifestyle. My daughter began incessantly talking about her "need" for a Frappuccino. She wanted one every day before and after school, late night after football games, while out shopping on the weekend, and any other time her emotional state deemed it necessary. She asked for Starbucks gift cards for her birthday and Christmas, and once she had a job, she began spending a good portion of her paychecks on her Starbucks habit. If we wouldn't take her to Starbucks, she would find a friend who would. At 500+ calories, 17 grams of fat, and $6 a pop, I could not believe how many Venti Caramel Frappuccinos she was consuming.

She had zero self-control. The reward center of her brain exploded with pleasure after the first taste, and seemingly in an instant, she became a slave to the chemical rush. As rudimentary and almost silly as it sounds to say, it all happened so fast. I didn't warn her ahead of time of the potential to become "hooked" on Frappuccinos and the importance of self-control, nor did I provide any guidelines for safe consumption or boundaries for Starbucks spending. It just didn't occur to me.

Just as Frappuccinos can be pleasurably addictive, so can smartphones and devices. It somehow doesn't cross parents' minds to establish a firm standard and healthy boundaries because children have grown up around these devices. Similar to how I naïvely introduced my daughter to Starbucks, parents are blindly giving new smartphones and devices to their children without warnings, limits, or safeguards.

The crucial problem is that without concrete warnings and limits, children become hooked on the dopamine rush occurring in their brains while using this technology. Because self-control is not taught or expected, it is not developed or exhibited.

An opportunity I believed to be a blessing to my child — a simple coffee date — contributed to weight gain and an unnecessary enslavement to a consumer product of this world. Once I recognized there was a problem, I was dumbfounded, asking myself, "Did I allow, or worse, encourage this new addiction?"

PARENTS AND SELF-CONTROL

Many parents buy their children a smartphone or device in an altruistic desire to bless them. It is easy to justify the decision as kids have grown up on this technology. Having their own phone is just the natural progression. After all, it is inevitable they will have one at some point. What is more, parents gain the immediate satisfaction and joy from pleasing their children. A child's elation at receiving their own smartphone makes it really hard not to feel like the greatest parent *ever*! This is a dangerously toxic feeling for parents. It feeds your desire to be liked, appreciated, and esteemed, while masking the grave need to issue to your child strong limits, warnings, and expectations.

You may begin with some type of phone contract for upholding expectations, but as time passes, rules fade, and boundaries blur. Even worse, in order to get the "greatest parent ever" feeling back, you allow your child to cajole you into letting them have all the apps and access they crave. By the time you discover a problem — pornography addiction, cyberbullying, sexting, or online relationships with strangers (to name only a few) — you are left completely shocked, dumbfounded, and fighting helplessness, while asking the same question I asked myself: Did I allow or encourage this? Powerless feelings of regret drown out all your rationale previously used to justify the child's limitless accessibility.

This is where I meet most parents: Swimming in shock at what they found on their child's phone, drowning in regret for not having protected them, and feeling powerless to change the situation.

Most parents hold a similar naive belief that kids can handle unlimited access on smartphones or devices and exercise self-control. They readily default to the assumption: if it's okay for me, it's okay for them. If adults can watch any genre of movies, play M-rated video games, access unfiltered Internet sites, or spend hours using social media — and experience no apparent negative effects — then surely kids can as well.

It's simply not true.

Children cannot handle all of this. Frankly, neither can adults, in my opinion. As you learned in Patience, the media they consume is rewiring their developing brains. They are becoming absolutely dependent on the dopamine rush generated by games, likes, shares, selfies, explicit pictures, and the constant feed of information. Just because it's not a cigarette, pill, or bottle doesn't mean the beautifully designed phones and tablets are any less addicting.

In the case of smartphones, parents must model the same self-control, healthy boundaries, and respect if they have any hope for their children to do the same.

We cannot teach what we cannot do ourselves. We'd be foolish to assume the addiction to media is happening only with children. Parents are susceptible and just as guilty. The introduction of smartphones seductively swept all of us — parents and children — off our feet. The question you must answer is: Have you regained your footing? Are you conscious of how much time you and your family spend on devices, or do you love them too much to care?

WE'D BE FOOLISH TO ASSUME MEDIA ADDICTION IS ONLY HAPPENING WITH CHILDREN.

We are raising our children in new and rugged territories. If you haven't found a stable footing of self-control, or you fail to recognize the dangerous terrain you are in, your children will be captured along with you.

Like a city that is broken down and without walls
(leaving it unprotected) Is a man who has no self-

control over his spirit (and sets himself up for trouble.)

Proverbs 25:28 (AMP)

A city without protection can be looted and plundered. A person without self-control welcomes the enemy's temptations and sets himself up for trouble. Self-control isn't solely to avoid overconsumption, obsession, or addiction. Self-control protects us from spiritual attack. Satan's mission is to steal, kill, and destroy, and nothing pleases him more than lack of self-control. His task is made simple when access to the spirit is easy.

Be self-controlled and alert. Your enemy the devil prowls around like a lion looking for someone to devour.

1 Peter 5:8

The devil prowls constantly looking for prey. Just like a lion, he circles, watching, and patiently waiting to pounce. Satan finds great satisfaction in finding prey who are pre-occupied, alone and unprotected — like parents and children whose spirits and souls are captivated, isolated, and distracted in the glow of their beautifully entertaining devices.

How do we protect ourselves from the devil's attacks? Self-control.

A lion's prey, for example an antelope, knows that being alert and aware of the surroundings provides protection. Antelope most often stay together in their herd. When a lion is seen, the antelope stares back at the lion acknowledging its presence and readying itself for potential attack. This is self-control exemplified. A learned skill of adaptation, self-control keeps them out of trouble.

Self-control is crucially important in our modern, screen-loving world because both parents and children alike are lacking the attention to and awareness of their surroundings. Too many are not looking up from their screens long enough to see the devil prowling nearby. Parents today are often unaware that their children have wandered off alone into a risky territory of the internet. There, the devil awaits to devour. Without a spirit of self-control, we will struggle to be alert for our children.

There are simple and practical ways parents can develop a spirit of self-control. For example, turn your phone off once all of your family is home for the evening and establish undistracted availability to your child. Take social media apps and games off your phone to reduce time-wasters. Cancel Netflix, if it mindlessly entraps you every day. Whatever it takes for you to activate a spirit of self-control, be brave and do it.

LEARNING THE LANGUAGE OF SELF-CONTROL

Self-control is the decision not to do something after thinking about doing it. It has been described as *"free won't"* — the opposite of free will. Learning to make a decision against our thoughts can be difficult and feel foreign to our human desires. It isn't something that will come naturally.

Similar to the continual practice and immersion it takes to learn a foreign language, self-control requires practice and awareness. The more dedicated a student is to learning vocabulary and immersing themselves in conversations, the more fluent in the new language they can become. Before long, the second language becomes as natural as the first. Acquiring self-control, like a foreign language, is not akin to learning to ride a bike, where you learn once and are set for life. Instead, self-control takes time and training. The nature of our instant and limitless culture saturates us, requiring the continual practice of self-control.

There are four concepts that can help your family learn self-control. They are like the beginning lessons of grammar and sentence structure when learning a new language. They set the foundation for all future learning. These four concepts — *Pre-Commitment, Limited Supply, Reduce the Allure, and Modify the Environment* — all work to set you up for self-control success.

Pre-Commitment

This is defined as making the voluntary decision to avoid access to temptation altogether. If you don't want the temptation to buy a fast-food hamburger for lunch, you pack a healthy alternative from home. If you don't want your children watching any television while they are young, you cancel your cable package. Essentially, it is simply making a wise decision in advance, so when the time comes, the wrong decision isn't made.

Setting up media standards is how you actively pre-commit your child to healthy media habits. You are choosing in advance how you want their character to be shaped, so that in moments of weakness, you don't give in to their desires. Whether the limit is for time allowed on video games or what type of apps are allowed, parents must own this type of pre-commitment for their children.

Furthermore, talk about pre-commitment with your child and how it looks in their life. A decision made in advance is the best way to set them up for success. Whether they pre-commit to media-related topics, simple daily tasks such as brushing teeth, when chores will be done, or even sexual purity, children can practice self-control.

Our culture at large does not teach children to pre-commit to any standards, morals, or habits. It preaches the message of immediate satisfaction and YOLO (you only live once) — things that require zero self-control.

Limited Supply

Research has shown that a person's supply of self-control is limited. Meaning, a person can exert only so much self-control before the supply is exhausted. In a famous 1998 study,[57] researchers sat two groups down in a room, each with two plates: one with freshly baked cookies and the other with radishes. They instructed one group to only eat the cookie plate and the other group to only eat the radish plate. Then they gave both groups an impossible puzzle to solve. Those who ate the radish plate and exerted self-control by not eating the cookies worked on the puzzle for only eight minutes before giving up. The group who ate the cookie plate and exerted zero self-control worked on the puzzle for nineteen minutes. The researchers concluded that after the radish-eating participants exerted self-control resisting the cookies, their self-control tank was diminished. They could no longer persevere through the hard puzzle task.

When children are expected to exert self-control in the classroom, on the playground, on the school bus, among peers, doing homework, and when playing with siblings, they deplete their self-control resources and are left with an empty tank. This is often why young children "lose it" once they come home from school. Their self-control tanks are bone dry from controlling themselves all day long.

What about older adolescents and teens? They, too, must maintain self-control during school, during extra-curricular activities, and among peers. Now, with the addition of their all-consuming and easily-accessible smartphones, they are expected to exert an entirely new level of self-control. A level that adults can barely attain, if we're honest. Knowing there is a limited supply, the question becomes,

"How do we set up teens for successful self-control?"

Parents must negate some of the situations where self-control is required by preventing the temptations altogether, thus maintaining a reserve of self-control. A great and applicable example in the context of media is the Internet. Avoid your child's temptation to get on, browse aimlessly, and potentially view inappropriate material by simply cutting off their unlimited access to the Internet. Remember, the devil prowls looking for someone to devour — someone who has an empty tank of self-control.

On phones and devices, you can disable the web browser, password-protect home computers, and install filters so no inappropriate material comes through. Too many parents feel it is an injustice to withhold the Internet from their children, expecting them to exert more self-control than they have the ability to do. Removing the temptation protects them and makes self-control easier.

When we acknowledge that our children have a limited supply of self-control, we can better understand how they will interact with media and the world around them. If basic self-control is a struggle, expecting appropriate self-control in an unlimited and open access media environment is plain foolish.

Reduce the Allure

We are often oblivious to the subtle messages fed to us that *more is better* and *now is better than later*. The effect on our children is grave, for they desire and truly believe that they deserve more right now. As parents, we have a monumental opportunity and responsibility to teach our children that *more* is not necessarily *better* and *later* can be better than now.

You are your child's role model. Our everyday behaviors can either reduce the allure and attractiveness of *more* and *now*, or they can increase *more* and *now's* attractiveness. If we always buy the newest iPhone the day it is released or spend an entire Sunday binge-watching Netflix, we tend to increase the allure of having *more* and doing it *now*.

However, if we prioritize our relationships above entertainment, live within our financial means, and delay gratification on a regular basis, we can reduce the allure of *more* and *now*.

What *we* prioritize, *our children* will learn to prioritize. What character virtues and values we hold, they will naturally hold as well. Therefore, if we truly desire for our children to possess self-control on screens, we must reduce the allure of screen obsession. This may mean not responding instantly to texts, not hyper-posting on social media, not checking email or news feeds every empty second, or even disconnecting for an entire day. The allure of *more* and *now* must be conquered with self-control.

> WE HAVE A MONUMENTAL OPPORTUNITY AND RESPONSIBILITY TO TEACH OUR CHILDREN THAT MORE IS NOT NECESSARILY BETTER AND LATER CAN BE BETTER THAN NOW.

Modify the Environment

If the environment within our homes is not conducive to self-control, we are setting ourselves and our children up for trouble. For example, if I try to give up my throughout-the-day Facebook habit, but the app is on my smartphone's home screen and my laptop's web browser opens with my Facebook feed, I'm doing no favors for my self-control. I must modify my daily routine and interactions if I have any hope of exercising self-control.

Consider your family's habits and environment regarding self-control. If television is your *more* and *now*, consider the environment. Does the flow of all your living spaces center around the television? Do you have televisions in every room? Do you have a television constantly on as background noise? Do you watch television while eating meals together?

Or perhaps smartphones are your family's love. Does everyone have their own phone and do their own thing on their phone when home together? Are phones allowed in the bedrooms? Do children walk around with headphones on to avoid communication? Are there any expectations for family dinners together without screens? Are parents just as guilty as kids for phubbing and deprioritizing relationships?

Before self-control can be exerted in media consumption or phone usage, the environment must be altered. Sell extra TVs, turn off cable programming, and rearrange furniture to create a setting that promotes talking to one another rather than focusing on the TV. Similarly, set new rules for phone use. Designate a basket for phones to be placed during dinner, for one hour after school, and at night to prioritize in-person communication.

Media environments directly affect media consumption. Parents must be alert, recognizing where self-control is lacking and then taking the lead to create a better environment for appropriate media use.

Following are a few practical and achievable ways to modify media behavior and environment both personally and for your family:

- Do not text or check email while your children are talking to you. Show your children they are more important than your phone by putting them first. If you must respond to something, communicate this with your child instead of allowing them to assume they are second to your phone.

- Turn off your television. Start with turning it off for one day and then two days and so on. If you lack of self-control and find yourself binge watching, consider canceling Netflix, Hulu, HBO, or cable TV.
- Designate specific times you will allow yourself to be on social media. Preferably, this time should be when children are in bed or actively engaged and will not feel neglected by you.
- Assign designated times to be "screen free." This can be dinner time, while driving around town (includes parents on phones and kids watching car televisions), or after a certain hour of the day. Screen-free family days and even screen-free vacations can be extremely valuable for building healthy relationships with children.
- Set 'do not disturb' driving restrictions on phones.

As your environment shifts and temptations are lessened, it is important to communicate the why and how with your child. Humbly convey the decisions you've made to build self-control and not conform to the media-consumed world.

LIMITED TIME & QUANTITY STANDARD

If given the freedom, children will choose candy over vegetables, video games over homework, and smartphones over sleep. Based on these choices, parents basically have two options. (1) Take away their free will and exercise self-control for them: *vegetables are the only option.* (2) Give them opportunities to practice self-control on their own: *finish homework before playing video games or lose video game privileges.* These parenting choices are not only to develop self-control, but they are also to protect your child's greater growth and development.

Considering the choices our children will naturally make, the standard to practice and develop self-control are **Limited time** and **Limited quantity**.

Limited Time

Limited time is placing blocks on certain hours when texting, WiFi, or data use are not allowed. This is where, as a parent, you exercise self-control for them. Given free will and unlimited access, most children will not exercise self-control on their devices. They will text throughout classes in school and stay up too late either online or texting. This standard protects their learning and sleep, helping them remain alert and self-controlled in other areas.

Most cellular service providers provide parental controls allowing for time limits for an additional monthly fee. These controls give parents the ability to set the exact time parameters when texting is allowed. At a minimum restrict texting, data and WiFi, during school hours and past bedtime. Rest assured, these limits will still allow for a 'white listed' group of contacts who can be texted anytime, regardless of time blocks. This can include mom, dad, grandma, neighbor, or other emergency contact your child may need. However, based on how many school administrators have told me, "It's most often the parents who are texting their kids all day long distracting them from class," we would be wise to limit ourselves in how often we contact them during school hours.

Both PC and Mac computers provide the ability to create individual user profiles and set up parental controls. These controls allow for daily time limits as well as time blocks or curfews, when your child is blocked from using the device. For detailed instructions visit: https://managingmediabook.com/resources

Some third party monitoring services, such as OurPact and TeenSafe, allow for time limits as well. Monitoring devices, such as Circle,

KoalaSafe, and Netpure enable limits to be set through the home's WiFi network. These limits can be beneficial to keep children from sneaking more screen-time than allowed or to block distractions during homework and studying hours.

When children have *Limited time* they are better protected from their own lack of self-control and from the devil's attacks. Setting these limits is a parent's way of being alert and aware of how smartphones and devices can easily consume a child and preventing this from happening.

Limited Quantity

Our society and its level of self-control changed when cellular service providers began offering unlimited texting. Suddenly, there was no need to self-regulate or limit how much and the quality of what was sent over text. The standard of *Limited quantity* is much needed to reset this imbalance. It will give your child the opportunity to exercise their own self-control. This is achieved by a *Limited quantity* of text messages. Quantity limits can also be established through cellular service providers. You can choose how many text messages your child can send/receive in one month.

Limiting your child's total quantity of text messages isn't simply a restriction; rather, it is a tool of empowerment. It provides an opportunity for your child to make the daily choice to exert self-discipline. In learning the foreign language of self-control, this is where they practice, practice, practice!

Here's how this works: You set a text limit and communicate the standard with the child. Tell them they have, for example, 1500 texts for the entire month, equating to 50 texts/day, and it is THEIR responsibility to exert enough self-control on a daily basis to make the texts last all month long. If they do not practice self-control, they will run out and have zero texts for the rest of the month.

Inevitably, every child assumes they "got this." When they run out of texts three-quarters of the way through the month, they quickly realize self-control takes effort and awareness. Once the monthly limit is reached, they can no longer send or receive and they feel the natural consequence of disconnection with their friends. A consequence they are empowered to avoid. Amazingly enough, their communication with friends doesn't end; it changes to phone calls. Phone calls can be a beautiful shift as they strengthen friendships with voice to voice communication and enhanced focus.

Similar to the *Limited time* standard, the 'white list' of contacts will still be able to send and receive from the child's phone even after the limit has been reached. Therefore, your communication with your child won't be cut off.

One caveat I do grant my children is when they can communicate with me why they ran out so quickly. Recently, one of my children was mentoring a younger friend. This young friend vented all of life's problems through hundreds of texts. Incoming texts count towards the monthly total and in a scenario like this, my child didn't want to freak out and tell the friend to stop texting. We granted more texts after hearing and reading their text conversations. We didn't want our child's ability to mentor and pour into others to be prohibited by their *Limited quantity*.

Quantity limits are the most openly discussed standard in our home because my children are actively engaged with it every day. I hear statements like, "I'm not going to respond to that and waste one of my text messages," and "I'm not going to waste my time or texts talking about stupid stuff." As the end of the month nears, I'll also hear, "I just received my AT&T text warning me I've used up 75 percent of my texts — I need to be careful to make sure I can make it 8 more days." This is the beautiful fruit of self-control. In a limitless landscape, they are practicing the skill of free won't — a skill that will translate into many other facets of life.

Furthermore, this standard reinforces the lessons of kindness, respect, and honesty. With a finite number of text messages, they learn to *make every text count*. If you have ever read a teen's text thread, you can appreciate how many one-emoji-face texts are sent, or the texts where they ask one another, "What do you want to talk about?....I don't know, what do you want to talk about?" I get it; they are kids. They are often silly while working out this digital communication skill. However, when it takes two or three text attempts to correctly spell a word they typed incorrectly, it's time they slow down and make it count.

As we discussed in the previous chapters, what you say matters and every word has impact. This lesson is huge and is reinforced with self-control! Texting grants the reader only one thing: words. Children need to learn to make every word count.

MORE PRACTICE

Despite our culture of cheapened and abbreviated communication between individuals, it is still possible to raise young men and women of high character — children who place value on self-control and their words. Children who are raised to speak words of life, to value honesty and wisdom, to hold their tongue when necessary, and to exert self-control in all aspects of their lives will be the world changers and kingdom expanders of the next generation.

Raising children of godly character means they must practice. The more they are immersed in character-building activities, the less foreign it will feel. Like a second language, it is all about immersion and practice.

Self-control can also be practiced through texting in the following areas:

1. **No texting people who are in the same room.** Have a real conversation instead!

2. **Reread what you typed and to whom you typed it before you hit send.** There is nothing worse than sending a text to the wrong person.

3. **Do not text "heyy" to every contact, looking for someone to respond and engage in a conversation to alleviate your boredom.** Boredom is okay and healthy.

4. **If you receive a text from an unknown contact, don't engage.** There is no need to continue a conversation for several messages trying to figure out who the person is or how you may know each other. Predators are real, and they know how to pull personal information from children.

5. **Text during appropriate times only.** If you have to sneak the phone during church to send the text, you shouldn't send it.

LIMITATIONS TO THIS STANDARD

Text messaging limits are best when instituted with the introduction of the first phone, as they set the standard for use from that point forward. If your child already has a phone, you may find it necessary to hit the "reset" button if obsessive texting affects their character.

For these children, begin the limit with a high number of texts and slowly walk them down to a reasonable level. Regardless, kids are super savvy and, as we've learned already, have nothing but time to figure out ways around our boundaries.

Listed below are a few ways *Limited Time* and *Limited Quantity* of texts may be thwarted:

iMessage

Texting quantity limits can be placed on an iPhone only if iMessage on an iOS is turned OFF and only SMS is allowed. iMessages travel through the "cloud" and are limitless. The only difference your child will notice here is green text bubbles instead of blue and they will not see the small "typing in progress" bubble when someone is responding.

Social media apps

As we discussed in the previous chapters, social media platforms grant the ability to communicate within the app. Your child could easily turn to one of these platforms to connect to and communicate with friends and to avoid running out of text messages. What may appear like amazing self-control may actually be rerouted communication.

Messaging apps

Also discussed in previous chapters, apps specifically designed to text and message over the internet instead of through cellular data can be used to thwart the self-control lesson.

Friends' phones

You may impose boundaries for your child's phone usage, but their closest friends may have zero boundaries or limitations. Because of this, your child may use their friends' phones to do what you are prohibiting. Even worse, the used phone "black market" in schools can easily supply your child with a device which can use texting apps over WiFi. Knowing this, I encourage you to either get rid of or lock up any old phones in your home.

WHY THIS IS VITAL

Here's the crux of self-control. This isn't just about my kids or my desire for them to have God-honoring character. I equally desire for your kids to express self-control as well. I want the teenager driving beside me on the highway to possess self-control. I want my children's friends, peer groups, and *most importantly*, their romantic interests to have self-control! This generation's self-control, or lack thereof, affects everyone, not just themselves.

> THIS GENERATION'S SELF-CONTROL, OR LACK THEREOF, AFFECTS EVERYONE - NOT JUST THEMSELVES.

This must be a combined effort — if not movement — from parents in the throes of raising children today. Lack of self-control is not an issue too big for a horde of parents to tackle.

We need this new standard to help our children learn what is foreign to them. As parents, we must create a dam to control the high-pressure flow of *more* and *now*. We must put restraints on over- indulgence, enlist limits on the limitless, modify our environments, abate the constant access, teach delay over instantaneous, and appropriately apply a child's limited supply of self-control.

And most importantly, we must be self-controlled and alert ourselves.

CHAPTER SIX

HUMILITY AND MODESTY:
No selfies, No MMS

The greatest ornament of an illustrious life is modesty and humility, which go a great way in the character even of the most exalted of princes.[58]

Napoleon Bonaparte

As a woman who does not watch television and relies on her husband to keep her updated on news events, I was very confused when I began hearing certain celebrity names thrown around in my various circles. My teenage daughters might mention them casually, or one of my friends would make a joke about them. I'd hear their names dropped on the radio, or I'd notice them splashed across a magazine cover as I loaded my groceries on the supermarket conveyor belt. While I was mildly curious, for the most part, I didn't care who they were. As a general rule, a precommitment to myself is that I try to stay away from celebrity anything — especially gossip.

After hearing a group of teenage girls ooh and ahh over how perfect and beautiful these women were, "omg they are totally #goals" (a slang term for one's desire to attain something similar), I confessed my ignorance to a friend. The level of worship these women received became disconcerting, and the Holy Spirit began waving warning flags at me. I assumed my friend would know who these women were, as her guilty pleasure is *People* magazine.

"Who on earth are these Kardashian people?" I finally asked in confession one evening.

"They are just rich girls with big boobs and butts and a reality show," she explained. I was unimpressed, but I inquired further.

"A reality show for what?" I asked. What could be so intriguing about their lives to evoke such immense worship and imitation?

My friend laughed and responded, as if realizing for the first time how silly the truth was, "Because they are rich and have big boobs." She didn't know if they had any extraordinary talents or achievements.

Primarily because I overheard my own daughters idolizing the Kardashian family, I decided to do some online research. It's absolutely possible I was the only thirty-something woman who had zero knowledge of this "dynasty." I may not need to explain the details regarding their fame, but for the sake of our topic, *humility and modesty*, I will highlight a few details, as they are central to our learning.

Born into money, the Kardashian girls grew up among the other rich and famous in Beverly Hills. The first three daughters born to Robert and Kris Kardashian are Kourtney, Kim, and Khloe. In 1991, the parents divorced and Kris married Caitlyn Jenner (formerly known as Bruce Jenner, the Olympic athlete). They had two daughters, Kendall and Kylie. After a homemade sex tape was "leaked" in 2007, Kim Kardashian's fame (and wealth) skyrocketed and landed her on the cover of *Playboy*. Just months later, her family had its own reality TV show, *Keeping Up with the Kardashians*.[59] Each hour-long episode showcases their rich girl problems — completely unrelatable to the common young woman watching the show. Their self-centered obsession with materialism trumps any family value they aim to portray. In 2010, the three older Kardashian sisters wrote an autobiography, *Kardashian Konfidential*, which hit the *New York Times* Best Sellers list.[60] In 2015, after her marriage to controversial rapper, Kanye West, Kim published her own book, *Selfish*, which quickly landed itself as a *NYT* best seller.[61]

This is where our Kardashian history lesson ends, because it was with Kim's book release that I began to learn about this family. *Selfish* features Kim's selfie photography. She is referred to as a "pioneer" and "trailblazer" for the selfie movement that has contaminated our culture. The Amazon.com book description states, "Kim has mastered the art of taking flattering and highly personal photos of oneself."[62] Kim is quoted as saying, "Selfies are the purpose of life."[63]

On Instagram, where Kim has over 100 million followers, she recently posted a nude picture with the caption, *"when you're like I have nothing to wear LOL"*. This photo garnered her 1.8 million likes and over 300,000 comments.[64]

Cue the record player screeching to an abrupt halt.

This is the woman I hear my daughters talk about? This is the kind of lifestyle our teenagers are setting as their goals for life? Seriously? This woman? A *Playboy* model? A woman who posts nude pictures on Instagram?

I cannot imagine a time growing up when I would have been allowed or encouraged to model my life and goals after a *Playboy* model/reality TV star turned pioneer of selfishness. I'm sure the '80s had its share of public sexuality scandals, but I never had access to them in my back pocket. *Playboy* models generally remained inside the shiny centerfolds of the magazine. This is such a far cry from my aspiration as a young girl to be like D. J. Tanner from Full House. Cute. Wholesome. Intelligent.

Now our young daughters, with access to everything and everyone, look up to Kim Kardashian. She has taught millions of girls that selfishness is okay, modesty is archaic, nudity is power, and humility is demonstrated through a lifestyle of "no regrets."

Heaven help us.

SELFIE-CENTERED

The social acceptance of self-portrait photography (thanks to our pioneer, Kim Kardashian) has transformed our culture. It began with the introduction of smartphones boasting high quality cameras and providing unlimited digital photos and a "self-portrait mode". Coupled with the explosive growth of social media, our culture has evolved into an epidemic of self-centeredness, self-promotion, and self-glorification. What is worse, all of these self-indulgences are for one purpose: worship. As Kim is worshipped on social and public media, young girls similarly seek to be worshipped through the accumulation of followers and likes.

Can we attribute all selfish-driven cultural issues to the rise of selfies? Certainly not, but one cannot deny that the selfie movement is promoting a gross social acceptance of self-centered living. Social media has long been the hub for selfie-sharing, but now everyday flaunting of life is normalized. Parents, including myself, are not immune. Boasting about possessions, life experiences, and perfect children is common practice among mothers on Facebook.

Like all generations who face large advancements and cultural shifts, our current problem is that we have no idea the true impact growing up in a selfie world will have on the iGen. What we do see right now, however, is this generation growing up idolizing Kim Kardashian and her nude selfies. One research poll found girls between 16-25 years old spend 48 minutes per day[65] practicing the fine art of self-portrait photography in order to get one perfect shot for Instagram. As the media defines beautiful with the Kardashians, every year we see teenage plastic surgery numbers rise[66] as young girls conform to this definition of beauty. Lip injections, breast augmentation, liposuction, and rhinoplasty have risen among teen girls.[67]   One Beverly Hills doctor further attributes this increase to the "selfie-stick" and smartphone apps which can alter images to create a different appearance.[68]

Let's identify some themes contributing to selfie-centeredness in this young generation. They only know life with WiFi, streaming television, and smartphone apps. Moreover, they now know porn as a household word and see marijuana as morally acceptable. Additionally, iGen, like the Millennials before them, are perpetually rewarded regardless of their performance, effort, or attendance. Albeit, many of these rewards are now in the form of likes, follows, and comments. This has led to a trend in college students unable to survive their freshman year amidst limitless distractions, college graduates unable to maintain a job where they aren't constantly praised, and new parents curating their newborn child's "brand" on social media before they learn to crawl.

Cultural influences aside, what is possibly most disheartening when examining the rise of selfie-centeredness are the parents' contributions. Selfish parenting attempts to maintain comfort at all costs. "If my child is comfortable and happy, then I am comfortable and liked." These parents work hard to maintain feelings of comfort in lieu of the hard work of discipline and creating character.

To maintain comfort, they are lax on chore requirements, throw wedding-caliber parties for every birthday and occasion, rush forgotten homework to school to avoid a bad grade, drive across town every night for select/club sports, write their child's college entry essays, defend their child against any adult or authority holding them accountable, and perpetually reward them with material things. Some call this helicopter or over-parenting, but what if the heart behind these actions isn't in our child's best interest — it's our own selfishness? After all, a happy and comfortable child sits in stark contrast to a child who experiences discipline and the discomfort of personal accountability.

If working hard to keep our children happy made parenting easy, who wouldn't do it? It's possible we are all a bit guilty of this.

SELFISH PARENTING ATTEMPTS TO MAINTAIN COMFORT AT ALL COSTS.

The problem is the long-term consequences of keeping our children happy and comfortable doesn't fall on us, as parents, but on our children, their bosses, coworkers, spouse, friends, and then, our grandchildren. No one else in our children's lives will ever work this hard for their maintained happiness. This causes their selfishness to intensify.

And when perpetual pleasure and constant comfort is an expected part of life, the best place to be fulfilled is on a device.

DEATH TO SELFIE; LIFE TO HUMILITY

*Do nothing out of selfish ambition or vain conceit.
Rather, in humility value others above yourselves, not
looking to your own interests but each of you to the
interests of others.*

Philippians 2:3-4

Jesus mastered the art of selflessness.

He would heal a person then humbly instruct the healed to tell no one. Despite being one with God the Father, He never demanded worship of himself. He rejected the popular crowd and chose to spend His time with the poor, the forgotten, and the sick. Jesus didn't see His own greatness as something to be flattered by, but instead He adorned others in the knowledge of their unique calling for His kingdom. He sought only the glory of His father.

For a country in which 75 percent of the population claims to be Christian,[69] Americans have strayed far from the likeness of Jesus Christ. Selfish ambition in today's culture is an honored virtue, touted as a character trait all should strive to attain. As a society, we've perverted this negative trait of selfish ambition by renaming it self-confidence and drive for personal success.

It's hard to consider the garnishing of likes, favorites, followers, and fame with the posting of self-portraits as anything *other than* selfish ambition.

James 3:16 states, "Wherever there is jealousy and selfish ambition, there you will find disorder and evil of every kind." This can easily be correlated to social media's negative effects. When the goal is to promote yourself and seek others' praise and worship for yourself, it is bound to lead to disorder (as seen in our mental health crisis: anxiety, depression, and bipolar) and evil of every kind (evident in cyberbullying, shaming, pornography, sex trafficking). With the sheer number of selfies and personal accolades posted over social media, there can be no denying that selfish ambition has become an accepted and normalized practice.

Selfish parenting embodies both jealousy and selfish ambition. "Momagers" (mom managers) mask their own underlying disorder with 'involved parenting.' We have this name, "Momagers," thanks to none other than Kim Kardashian's mom, Kris. This is the mom who is managing and manufacturing her child's selfish ambitions for them. Seeking the reflective glory of their children, "Momagers" devote themselves to successfully executing their children's popularity, talent, and opportunities. Mom fame is the new twist on selfish ambition characterized by making the child appear perfect, and, by association, the mom perfect too. A recent photo that went viral across social media depicts this trend perfectly. The photo was of a one-year-old's unicorn Halloween costume. Posted on the one-year-old's "official" Instagram account and the mom's Facebook, the caption read: *"The cutest unicorn in the land (two unicorn emojis) all handmade by mommy. I even baked the horn in the oven. #imsoextra."*[70]

Selfish ambition must be put to death in order to live a life of humility. We are guilty, not only of our own selfishness, but also for teaching it to our children. Our humility is just as needed in this world as our children's humility.

Our standard must always come back to Jesus. Our ambition should be to lead a life of humility as Christ himself did, continually denying personal glory in order to make much of God the Father. Our ambition should be to express the fruit of the Holy Spirit: love, joy, peace, patience, kindness, goodness, faithfulness, gentleness, and self-control (Gal 5:22-23) in contrast to the acts of the flesh, including selfish ambition (Gal 5:19-20). Our ambition should be to raise children who model the character of Jesus, instead of the character of popular culture. These ambitions should drive us to maintain a higher standard for raising our children.

Therefore, we must provide the most conducive environment for humility and the fruit of the Spirit to flourish. As parents, we must uphold a standard that denies selfish ambition. If selfish ambition and self-centeredness breed when we focus on self, we must change the environment. The standard we set to build a character of humility is *No selfies*. That is, no pictures taken of oneself solely for the purpose of self-promotion.

THE STRUGGLE OF NO SELFIES

So far, all of the character-trait waters we have entered have been fairly shallow. It's easy to get our feet wet on the zero-entry beach of patience and respect before we float in inner tubes through the waist-deep waters of kindness and honesty. These character traits are fundamentally and socially expected and necessary for personal development. In other words, neither your child nor you should feel like you are drowning while building patience, respect, kindness, honesty, and to some extent, self-control.

Humility and modesty, however, find us in the roughest waters. No dipping your toes into shallow zero-entry and definitely no casual floating. In fact, it is probably more akin to white water rafting in icy cold waters where you must paddle against the current to reach land.

Who's in?

Well, like it or not — you're in these waters. Parents and children alike are neck-deep in the rapids. Our view of where we are left treading water shows a steep and raging waterfall just shortly ahead of where the current flows. Consequently, the choices before us are: (A) to fight the current and persevere towards land, or (B) go with the flow and let the waterfall take and potentially crush us.

Indecision at this point will lead us straight over the waterfall of self-centeredness, and the reality is that no one knows what lies at the bottom of the fall. The selfie trend is too premature to predict its final outcome. Will the character of our children withstand the turbulent and high pressure waters, or will their self-centered focus leave them broken and damaged?

Enforcing *No selfies* in order to build humility is choosing to swim towards land. It will be exhausting to swim against the current since you must force your child to swim with you. They will rarely choose to swim towards land as their peers passively head over the waterfall. In fact, they may fight so hard against you, it feels like you are drowning as you carry them along. Can you picture this?

We must remember what lies ahead if we persevere: character! Humility is worth fighting for, and this land of character we swim towards is closer than you know. If you are already in the water, isn't it worth trying to reach land?

Humility is absolutely worth the struggle and exhaustion.

I concede that when you implement the standard of *No Selfies*, your child will try to convince you that they are dying a slow and painful death of social humiliation. "But I've seen tons of selfies posted on Instagram that were taken at the waterfall. They got tons of likes because it's gorgeous, and those people seem just fine!" Go ahead and laugh. You know the "but everyone else" excuses are coming.

Communication is essential here. In order for them to accept (or at least respect) your rule of *No selfies*, they must first understand what humility is and why it is important. Don't assume they know; they've grown up surrounded by selfishness. Humility isn't a trait they are bound to know. Explain that humility is thinking of yourself less often and how that is generally impossible when the camera is in self-portrait mode all day long. Also describe what humility is not. It is not thinking less of yourself, "No one will ever like me, I'm worthless," nor is it arrogant boasting about yourself, "Everyone knows I have the most Instagram followers because my story is lit." On the contrary, humility is holding a modest opinion of your importance, "I may have scored the only touchdown, but I couldn't have done it without my team." As you define humility, provide your child with practical examples for their own life, so they can begin to understand how it is displayed.

Furthermore, express your conviction to raise them to embody the words of Philippians 2:3-4: "Do nothing out of selfish ambition or vain conceit. Rather, in humility value others above yourself…" What does it mean to *value others above yourself?* If you can, provide examples of how your child is already doing this well. Ask your child if they can identify areas of their own selfish ambition. In the same way, humble yourself and admit your own selfish ambitions as we all have them. Discuss how unhealthy media habits contribute to characteristics and behaviors that distance our heart from God's.

As you discuss the standard of *No selfies*, be open to hear their thoughts, concerns, and heart on the topic. Their feelings and emotions regarding this topic are very real to them, and they deserve empathy. An authentic discussion will do more for their character than an argument where you win.

Communication alone will not stop them from taking selfies. Other than disabling the camera, there is no restriction you can activate on a phone or device to stop your child from taking pictures of themselves. This is a good-faith standard. Spot checks of photo apps or the camera roll are necessary for accountability. Generally speaking from my own experience, you'll never find just one selfie. You'll find a batch of them — ten to twenty selfies taken from different angles, with slightly different head positions and smiles, all captured on a particular day she is feeling pretty or he is feeling "swol" (slang term for muscular or buff).

With *No selfies* as a stated expectation, any discovered selfies should be immediately addressed. Choose a tangibly felt consequence, such as disabling the camera for one week or one month, depending on the quantity and inappropriateness of the selfies you find. At the same time, talk about it with your daughter (or son, but most often this will happen with the girls). By all means, compliment her, if indeed, she looked beautiful that day, but aim to discover her heart behind the photos. What was she planning to do with these selfies? How do these strategically taken self-portraits contribute to her self-worth and confidence? The child will most often attempt to justify, "It's just a few pictures. What's the big deal?" Humility is the big deal — not in this world, but certainly with Jesus.

Additionally, your child will try their best to convince you that they cannot survive without their camera. It's true that teachers today capitalize on the fact most students have smartphones with cameras and may ask your child to use their camera for class-related purposes. However, I have never found a school where it is a requirement. Schools will always provide alternative resources to accomplish assignments.

Be brave and keep life in proper perspective. Children have survived for thousands of years without phones or cameras. Our world is not so technologically evolved that pencil and paper are an artifact in museums. They can just as easily handwrite the day's notes as they can snap a picture of it. If nothing else, consider that learning is lost when notes are photographed for reference instead of handwritten for retention. Adapting to life without a camera is a natural repercussion that flows from your standard and expectations. It reminds your child that the camera is a privilege, not a right. This privilege comes with responsibility and an expectation of humility.

One final consideration, regarding smartphone cameras, is the ability children have to take photos and videos of *everything*. Whether to capture the next viral video or to *record* something to prove it happened, the propensity to record life instead of *live* life is skewing our children's reality. Children are facing expulsion from schools or criminal charges because of inappropriate use of their smartphone camera. Plain and simple, if you find anything alarming in the camera roll, disable the camera.

MODESTLY TEXTING

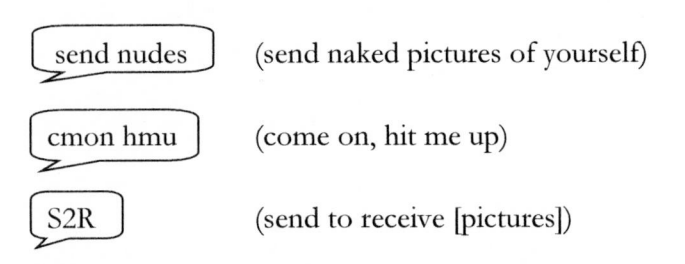

send nudes   (send naked pictures of yourself)

cmon hmu   (come on, hit me up)

S2R   (send to receive [pictures])

These are common texts you may read on your child's phone. The sending and receiving of nudes, generally referred to as sexting, is now a common way children express themselves. When I have seen these types of solicitations on my daughters' phones, they are most often from boys who are not even current romantic interests of my girls! They are from regular boys, motivated by pornography, who thought they'd ask and see what happens. Other times they are from boys whom my daughters are only "talking to" in a get-to-know-you sort of way.

It's not hard to surmise how a relationship will end up when the get-to-know-you conversation starts with "send sexy pic." Sadly, in our sexually explicit culture, nude photos aren't just of girls anymore. "dic pics" as they are called are shared equally from boys to girls. The constant social pressure to send pictures can crack the strongest of foundations and convictions in a young person.

These are not the type of social stresses we had growing up. Our children are playing an entirely new game of manipulation with ever-changing rules of play. One common manipulation play begins when a girl refuses to send nude photos. To deflect rejection, the boy retaliates by spreading humiliating rumors, usually sexual in nature, around school and on social media in order to shame the girl. However, if the girl concedes and sends a nude photo, the boy may share the photo with friends or online websites to "slut-shame" her. Smartphone apps, such as *Secret Photo Calculator Plus*, allow for photos and videos to be hidden and password protected. These apps can serve as warehouses for teen boys gathering explicit photos as a display of notoriety, power, or popularity.

Sexting scandals are almost commonplace in American middle schools today; however, it's a sick, degrading game played all over the world. Recently, Fight the New Drug, a non-profit dedicated to raising awareness on the harmful effects of pornography, shared a report from Australia where more than 2,000 images were posted or traded on a website that targeted specific schools and individual girls. Full names of girls being "hunted" appeared on a "wanted" list where users could contribute more identifying information about the girl such as school, home address, or phone number. When nudes were acquired, "wins" as they call them were uploaded or offered in exchange for a trade.[71]

This ties into another game that is played: sextortion. This is when a predator begins an online relationship with a young girl or boy. Most often, the predator gathers personal information from social media sites in order to feign relevance or commonality. After a grooming process to build trust, the predator asks for nude pictures or videos. Once the predator acquires one picture, he asks for more and threatens to spread the pictures he has on the Internet or directly to friends and family, unless he receives more. Some predators aren't acting on their own, but as part of a larger network aiming to extort money or even traffic their victims.

As if this isn't bad enough, the twisted game of sextortion has recently evolved into "revenge porn." This game is typically played after a breakup. The explicit photos or videos taken or shared during the relationship are posted on defined "slut-shaming" or "revenge porn" websites along with the person's name or other identifying information. Some women who are dragged into this game have legally changed their names to escape the repercussions.

We are foolish to believe that any child with a smartphone isn't on the sidelines, waiting to get in the game. They don't know how brutal the games are; they just followed their crowd of friends into the arena. Even if they do know the games and their risks, children tend to optimistically believe they'll play for *fame* instead of *shame* — an extremely dangerous gamble.

No loving parent would ever intend for their child to play these aforementioned games, much less even be near the sidelines vying for a chance to participate. Unfortunately, our good intentions have been outpaced by the explosive technological advances of the Internet and media. Now, in the same way parents intend for their child to avoid dangerous, life-threatening situations, such as drunk driving or drug use, they must intend for them to avoid these games of sexual manipulation.

Modesty is defined as "behavior, manner, or appearance intended to avoid impropriety or indecency."[72] When we consider that modesty is behavior *intended to avoid*, we can assume it is a preventative and proactive behavior. It is a choice made in advance — a pre-commitment — to evade immorality, arrogance, and vanity. This is not a behavior that develops accidentally; rather, it is taught, modeled, and expected.

Modesty is neither archaic nor negative. It can no longer be viewed as overprotective, over-conservative or even meek. When modesty is devalued, immorality spreads. We must regain our faith in the value and benefits of this character strength. We can define modesty with a smartphone as: behavior intended to avoid sexually explicit photos and videos being sent, received, or uploaded.

Smartphones and media have changed the game. You cannot afford to remain ignorant or assume your child will never get involved. Every child with a smartphone or internet access is inside the arena. Any indecision or failure to intentionally keep your child off the field can land them directly in the game's starting lineup. These sexual manipulation games of today, like the Gladiator games of the first century, are entertainment at the expense of an innocent victim.

WHEN MODESTY IS DEVALUED, IMMORALITY SPREADS.

If you intend to avoid his participation or her broken reputation, you must reconsider their vulnerability to join these games. More specifically, you must take the intentional steps necessary to avoid inappropriate material sent and received. The standard to protect and build your child's modesty is **No MMS (Multimedia Messages)**, otherwise known as *No sending or receiving pictures.*

No sending or receiving pictures is a choice to keep your child off the field and out of the arena. This is a pre-commitment standard you choose for your child until they reach an age when you believe they are mature enough to choose modesty on their own. In my experience, this maturity rarely occurs during middle school. They will be challenged by this standard, not because they desire to send explicit content, but because they will not be able to send any pictures or videos. Your daughter won't be able to send you a picture of a dress she found shopping for your approval. Your son will not be able to receive a picture of a homework assignment he missed due to a doctor's appointment. Knowing and understanding the risks associated with the game, however, must drive you to choose what they *need* over what they *want*.

Trust is a vital aspect in a healthy relationship with your child. However, trust within the context of a smartphone or device means you aren't just trusting your child — you are trusting the world's access to your child. Trust is important, but knowledge and wisdom are crucial.

If you question whether this standard is too controlling based on the modesty and trustworthiness your child already possesses, consider a few questions. Bear in mind what we learned in Chapter 5: children have a limited supply of self-control.

Do you trust what everyone will send to your child? And let's be realistic: if kids have the audacity to solicit pictures, they will apply the same audacity to sending them unsolicited.

Is "slut" an identity you wish for your daughter? A young girl's heart's desire is to be loved, cherished, and desired. She can easily believe sending one picture will lead to fulfillment of this desire, but one picture, one share, or one upload can remain on the internet forever. Likewise, the shame can live forever in her heart.

Would you willingly allow your son to "hunt" for wanted nudes of girls? One word: testosterone. Teenage boys have up to 50 times the amount of testosterone produced during puberty, than any time prior in their lives.[73] This can cause a teenage boy's brain to become consumed with sex. Combine today's technology with a male's instincts, and you risk this type of immoral behavior.

How much temptation can your child withstand? Is your child strong enough to resist sending the nude pictures being asked of them — even if it is from their long term romantic interest? Can they endure the bullying or shaming that comes with refusing? Can they resist the urge to look if friends forward on the most recent nude pictures they received?

How will viewing inappropriate or pornographic material change your child's view of the opposite sex or even the act of sex itself? Pornography is shaping young men's and women's views of one another into an ugly parody of what God intended. Sexuality has become something to exploit, rather than cherish. How will inappropriate pictures shape your children's perspective of relationships, marriage, and sex?

Why risk your child's purity, propriety, and reputation at the hands of preteen and teenage children who have undeveloped frontal lobes, raging hormones, and an inability to comprehend future consequences? This standard gives your child an immediate response to nude requests, "My parents disabled my ability to send and receive pictures." No thought or consideration is required of them — something my own daughters have confessed they appreciate.

We cannot assume *stuff like this doesn't happen,* or worse, *it isn't a big deal if it does.* Tween and teen sexting is child pornography, and it cannot be ignored.

TURNING ON MODESTY; TURNING OFF PICTURES

Modesty is not only about your desire to keep nude photos of your child off the internet. Modesty is about teaching them to honor God with their body. As the parent and Christ follower, you must illustrate why this type of protection is important for developing the character God desires.

In the first letter to the Corinthians, Christ followers are exhorted to — "Flee from sexual immorality." Not only because it is a sin "against your own body," but because "your body is a temple of the Holy Spirit, who is in you, whom you have received from God."(1 Cor 6:18-19) All practical implications for sexual immorality aside, this is a command from the Word of God. "Honor God with your body." (1 Cor 6:20) If you are raising your child to be a disciple of Jesus, you should not allow them to disobey this command. Further driving the importance of this command into believers, Hebrews 12 says: "See to it that no one misses the grace of God...See that no one is sexually immoral." (v 15-16). This is our job as parents: to see to it, that our children are not given the opportunity to be sexually immoral.

This is much easier said than done in today's culture. The *No sending or receiving pictures* standard will require good communication for there to be understanding of God's expectation for modesty. Your standard and values will conflict with everything they see among their friends and peers. As you prepare to disable their ability to utilize this common smartphone feature, engage in conversations to turn on modesty. Here are a few examples:

What do they know? What have they seen?

Ask what they've seen and heard in school and throughout culture about sexting and pornography. Have they had friends send or receive nude pictures or experiment with porn? If so, what were the consequences? Did it end well? Encourage her to think of future consequences from participating in the sharing of nude photos. If she cannot think of any, be sure to provide some possibilities (i.e. chronic fear/anxiety that everyone in school or town has seen her naked, or college administrators discovering her picture on line when considering admission).

> MODESTY IS ABOUT TEACHING THEM TO HONOR GOD WITH THEIR BODY.

Real discussions about sexting need to be frequent and frank. This may feel uncomfortable at first. Don't be afraid to use the lingo they use and point-blank ask them what they've seen. It is better to address the "elephant in the room" than to act as though it isn't there. Your openness to talk about real issues will provide safe space for them to be real.

Why is sexting so prevalent?

Foremost, if your child has a limited understanding of sexual attraction, this will need to be elaborated on. For both sons and daughters, describe how God created boys to be more visually stimulated than girls. A teenage boy doesn't crave long romantic conversations; they would prefer to look at a girl. Because of boy's visual nature, they believe girls are equally visually stimulated as well.

This is one reason why boys are sending unsolicited "dic pics" to girls. In contrast, however, God created girls to crave love and conversation more than visual stimulation. This is why smooth, sweet, and complimentary words sent over text can easily coerce a young girl's heart to send nude pictures.

Explain to your child how sexting's prevalence is partially because of opportunity and partially because it is considered the "safest" way to engage sexually with someone. Smartphones make taking and sending these pictures easy, and in a generation who already avoid face-to-face interactions, sexting is considered a logical next step. It could be said, sexting is the impersonal way of "hooking up". Make certain they know that nothing sent over text or the internet ever disappears. Apps like Snapchat, where the photo disappears, lure children to believe it is safe or won't be shared — which is rarely the case. Also, explain to them how difficult it is to un-see a picture they've already seen.

How does it affect character?

These discussions provide a great opportunity to connect the character trait "dots" in order to see the big picture of why character is so important. Explain how a boy's selfishness gives rise to desire and perceived entitlement to a nude picture. A young girl's limited supply of self-control and lack of self-respect leads her to consent and share a nude photo. Unkindness and dishonesty lead the boy to share the photo publicly. One negative character trait compounds another, leading to disaster. A simple Google search for news stories involving sexting provides a plethora of these modesty fails and the repercussions that followed.

These conversations will also help you gauge their appreciation for modesty. Often, the lack of respect for the Internet's power and reach causes children to have no fears. Without a healthy fear of their nude photos being shamed or spread, they will act on their impulses. Your role is to educate them in a way that establishes a healthy understanding (fear) of future consequences. Because even if you disable their ability to send and receive, they can still send and receive from their friends' unrestricted phones, if they really wanted to.

This standard must coincide with education; otherwise, it doesn't develop modest character. Unfortunately, these conversations need to begin before middle school. Children, on an average, receive their first smartphone at the age of ten, thus sexual manipulation games are bleeding into our elementary schools. These young ones may not be taking provocative pictures; instead, they may be taking screen-shots of pornographic content and sending it unsolicited to their contacts.

Similar to *No selfies* to develop humility, *No sending or receiving pictures* is also a good-faith standard. Unfortunately, this is not a password protected feature within iOS or Android. Because your child could turn this feature back on, your conversations and accountability are essential. Otherwise, once they discover how to turn it back on, they will constantly contend with the temptation to deceive you when they desire to send a picture.

How you enforce this depends on your parenting style. For my family, once we discussed God's command and our heart for them to avoid these sexually immoral games, we established the standard with firm boundaries. Enabling MMS in order to send or receive pictures over text would result in losing the privilege of the smartphone for a period of time. This is enforced through our routine checks of their phones. Software used to find deleted text messages can also retrieve deleted pictures. Since our children know we can find anything deleted, this hasn't been a huge struggle. Accountability keeps them honest and modest. One of my daughters even responded to requests for pictures with, "I don't do that, and you shouldn't either." They may not have liked the standard at first, but seeing the calamity sexting has brought on their friends and peers has made them thankful.

If you don't establish a foundation of what is safe, right, healthy, and moral, the world will convince your child that inappropriate material is perfectly acceptable. Modesty is taught through communication and relationship, but it is protected through parental intentionality. Until the child's frontal lobe can appreciate modesty, parents must make purposeful decisions to honor modesty.

CAVEATS TO THE STANDARD

Lest I leave you in complete despair, there are a few caveats to this standard. These are gray areas where modesty and humility can still be preserved and your child can build responsibility and trust.

Groupies: I define Selfies as individual pictures taken for the sake of showing off oneself. A picture taken in the same fashion but with a group of friends is considered a "groupie." These pictures are allowed and even encouraged as it documents moments in relationship with other people. The goal isn't to squash your child's fun and memories, but to keep the focus on others instead of themselves.

Tourist Attractions: When you are standing somewhere meaningful and want to remember that you were there, a selfie gets it done. The key is staying humble and taking it for yourself, not for bragging or boasting purposes. The new trend of "if you don't post it, it never really happened" is a lie you must debunk.

Email Pics: There are times when children can benefit from the functionality of sending and receiving pictures (homework, extra-curricular involvement, etc.). In these instances, emailing pictures can work quite well. Most kids today are not willing to share selfies or explicit pictures over email for fear of who may see it. Texts and social media, for whatever skewed reason, are perceived as completely acceptable for sending and sharing nudes.

I cannot stress enough the benefit of teaching your child values versus allowing the world to brainwash them. Degrading your values in order to make parenting easier will produce lackluster adults who cannot reconcile the Christian in the Bible with cultural Christianity. As radical as the idea of limiting your child in this way may seem, they desperately need to see modesty and humility as valued characteristics.

Training and teaching your children takes time, intentional thought, action, and perseverance. Yes, it is hard! But our charge as followers of Christ and parents is this: to make disciples. The values and morals we have as disciples must cross over into the technology and media we engage with.

CHAPTER SEVEN

Self-Worth:

Delay social media access

Over the years, I've interviewed thousands of people, most of them women, and I would say that the root of every dysfunction I've ever encountered, every problem, has been some sense of a lacking of self-value or of self-worth.[74]

Oprah Winfrey

"Mom, is there anything I can do to earn twenty dollars today? I really need to get my nails done."

It was a Sunday afternoon, and my fourteen-year-old daughter was pleading with me out of her profound desperation to have her fake nails filled in at the nail salon. This luxury is not one I financially support; therefore, it was her responsibility to find babysitting jobs and save her money to maintain "properly" manicured nails. She had already mowed the yard, but she was still $20 short of what she needed.

I looked at her and felt compassion. I was proud that she was willing to work for the money and not simply whine about how cruel we are for not giving her $20. She didn't even ask to borrow the money, already knowing we expected her to earn the money herself. She needed the money fast, as I am only willing to drive to the salon on Saturdays and Sundays — and Sunday was passing quickly.

"Okay," I started with an affirmative yet jovial tone, "write a five-hundred-word essay on what it is like being a teenager without any social media. Advantages and disadvantages. I will pay you twenty dollars."

Her disgusted look displayed her inner conflict. She jeered, "You cannot be serious, Mom."

"Oh, I am absolutely serious. What is it worth to you? Twenty dollars and a ride to the salon?" I silently thanked the Lord for this divinely inspired idea. I was fairly confident she'd end up writing the 500 words, and I hoped this opportunity to personally reflect and evaluate her circumstances would ignite an understanding of why she was restricted from using social media. I prayed for the Holy Spirit to move in her heart.

Less than one hour later, she presented me with 500 words — precious gems, as I refer to them — written from the overflow of the heart and mind of a teenager prohibited from using social media. With her permission, here is a small passage that so poignantly depicts what my words cannot.

> "One advantage I would say I have over my
> girlfriends is that they easily conform and freely
> give in to sexual desires. They do not think about
> any future consequence, and they think this is all
> okay, while I disagree. If I relied on social media

for answers to whether or not these things were okay or appropriate, I would get a lie saying it was all right to do. So when my friends come to me at school wanting to talk to me about these things, I don't tell them everything is okay because that would be lying. I simply ask if they are happy and satisfied for longer than just one day or a couple of hours. They are always searching for something to make them happy and whole. They are never satisfied . . ."

WORTH

One of the most important characteristics in all of human character is self-worth. It is defined as "the sense of one's own value or worth as a person."[75] The opposite, you could say, is finding oneself *worthless*.

Self-worth is confidence in knowing we were masterfully created for a purpose. It is what enables us to believe we are not only capable of doing far more than we could dream or imagine, but that we are also worthy of these things. Self-worth drives decisions and influences our convictions. At the foundation, self-worth is defining yourself by who you are in Christ.

SELF-WORTH NEEDS NO VALIDATION FROM ANYONE OR ANYTHING.

Self-worth is not living with constant doubt and making decisions based on fears. Self-worth needs no validation from anyone or anything, as it is defined by the Creator and accepted by oneself.

While people and external forces can certainly influence self-worth, discovering one's worth is a personal and solitary journey. Furthermore, self-worth has no currency. It cannot be quantified by anyone or anything.

I am raising children who, due to trauma and neglect, had very little self-worth. As their mother, I long to hand self-worth over like a gorgeously wrapped present that they tear open, put on, and immediately rejoice in. Unfortunately, this character trait is rebuilt slowly and over a long period of time. Frankly, it doesn't seem fair how quickly self-worth can be stolen, yet how slowly it replenishes. Self-worth itself, therefore, is of high worth and should be protected from loss, theft, or destruction — especially in the self-identifying teenage years.

THE SELF-WORTH THIEF

Picture a beautiful resort where you and all your friends meet up routinely. The environment is always energetic and dynamic, providing opportunities to catch up with friends. The food is amazing; perfectly prepared every time. The music is always original, and the entertainment never fails to delight.

There is only one problem at your resort. There is a thief who sneaks in unbeknownst to everyone. You feel like you are missing something, but you can't figure out what it is. Most of you don't realize you have been robbed until after you leave, and then it's too late. This causes conflicted emotions to rise. You love the resort and everything it offers, but you hate leaving yourself exposed and vulnerable. This thief is ruthless and truly makes you question if the resort is worth it.

Welcome to social media, the go-to resort of millions.

156

We connect, share, like, comment, watch, listen, and learn. Meanwhile, the devil subtly steals our self-worth.

> *The serpent was the shrewdest of all the wild animals the LORD God had made. One day he asked the woman, "Did God really say you must not eat the fruit from any of the trees in the garden? . . . You won't die!" the serpent replied to the woman.*
>
> *"God knows that your eyes will be opened as soon as you eat it, and you will be like God, knowing both good and evil."*
>
> *The woman was convinced.*
>
> *She saw that the tree was beautiful and its fruit looked delicious, and she wanted the wisdom it would give her. So she took some of the fruit and ate it.*
>
> Gen 3: 1, 4-6

The woman was convinced. Just like that. It only took Eve's gaze to settle upon something beautiful that she didn't possess to convince her. A few persuading questions and she forgot the truth, her value and how perfect life was. Her high value to her Creator was questioned. Her self-worth was stolen. Satan knew exactly how to deceive her: with lies and through her eyes.

Deception from the enemy nearly always involves twisted truths and desirable visuals. In Matthew 4, Satan tempts Jesus in the wilderness. After failing at his attempt to convince Jesus to prove He was the Son of God, by turning stones into bread and jumping off a high point of the city and saving himself, Satan makes one last attempt. He shows Jesus all the kingdoms of the world and their glory and offers them all to Jesus in exchange for His worship (vv. 8-9). Jesus then casts the devil away (v.10).

Jesus is our perfect example. He stood strong in who He was and His purpose on earth. No tempting visual or deception promising something better would deter Him.

But we are far more bent to be easily deceived like Eve.

Social media is akin to the most spectacular resort you have ever experienced. So much to do and see, there hardly seems enough time to take it all in. Satan takes your pleasure and then positions himself to persuade you:

> Scrolling through Instagram, you see a picture of your friend's children. They look perfectly behaved playing outside, without a speck of dirt on their clothes. You tap "like" then wonder, "Why can't my kids be this way?" Almost instantly, Satan walks through the open door and slams you with negative thoughts about your parenting abilities and your children's behavior. These thoughts take root, and you become bitter toward your children because they don't look or act like your friend's children.

> You see a video advertisement shared on Facebook for a new product to make your neck look skinny and reduce flab. You ponder, "Who buys this? I don't think my neck needs to be skinnier!" But then you pass a mirror, and subtle doubts enter through the window of opportunity left open by the video. The doubts take root, and you become fully convinced your neck is a wrinkled, saggy mess.

> The famous or pseudo-famous people you follow on Twitter always seem to be out doing fun stuff, so you determine you

should do the same. After all, you have thousands of followers. "You're just as famous," Satan whispers. You drop thousands of dollars you don't really have for that boat you have always wanted, so you, too, can live like that. You post your pictures from your adventure on the lake, but somehow you get only twelve likes. A stark contrast to the 12K likes your celebrity inspiration had. Unlike the celebrity, you still have fifty-nine payments left.

Even if I didn't hit on your specific niche of deception, you get the idea. We see; we compare. We see; we doubt. We see; we covet. This is how the enemy works. He shows us what we do not or cannot have, whispers lies, and thus convinces us these things are of the greatest value. Every time we are deceived, the enemy wins. Almost humorously, the constant deception Satan uses is precisely what social media platforms exploit to make money.

And this is an adult's perspective. A teenager, whose self-worth is still being molded and solidified, stands in even greater danger of theft.

I'm very much aware that there are a plethora of eight- to twelve-year-olds who regularly use social media. However, all popular social media platforms have at least a minimum age of thirteen due to federal laws prohibiting data collection from minors. Because of this, I will refer to all children on social media as teenagers — 13 or older. If you have allowed social media access under thirteen, the rest of this chapter most certainly still applies to your child.

SOCIAL MEDIA AND TEENS

If you, as an adult, can recognize how social media threatens your own self-worth and confidence, the question we cannot be afraid to ask is: What impact and effect will the social media culture have on my teen? *Perhaps the problem isn't asking the question, but accepting the answer.*

Let's dive into the murky waters of our teenager's world. The teenage brain works differently from ours, so we must have a clear picture of how they view and interact in this realm. For most teens, social media is where they live. As in, this is their second reality, where they communicate with peers — friends, foes, and strangers alike. It is a reality they get to create. If they don't like their real self, they can easily create a new identity in the social media world. Moreover, they can create multiple personas across multiple platforms in order to be whomever the world wants them to be at any moment. The pictures they post and the words they write allow them to slip in and out of different personalities and identities, trying them on as they would an article of clothing.

The word *communicate* is used loosely with this age group because these conversations are happening through screens and lack critical tone and nonverbal cues. The screen provides "digital courage" for teens to say anything without any thought of consequence. Whether in hate or in lust, words flow from the fingertips of teens who would rarely find the fortitude to say it face-to-face.

In her book, The Big Disconnect, Dr. Catherine Steiner-Adair says this about communication:

> "There's no question kids are missing out on very critical social skills. In a way, texting and online communicating — it's not like it creates a nonverbal learning disability, but it puts everybody in a nonverbal disabled context, where body language, facial expression, and even the smallest kinds of vocal reactions are rendered invisible."[76]

When communication exists primarily at this digital level, social skills are impaired. A teen's second reality never quite fits into their real world, leaving them feeling lost and disconnected. For example, when a conflict arises between two friends in the cafeteria, they turn to social media to air their grievances instead of talking through the problem — where both verbal and nonverbal communication could resolve and redeem the situation.

Perhaps where this is most poignantly displayed is in romantic relationships. A relationship that begins between screens and on social media tends to move from zero to nudes in a day. However, when these same teens come face-to-face, all the shared intimacies and courageous words sent behind the screens prove to have no foundation. The bravado from which they typed is not equal to the valor necessary to speak directly to each other. At the core, these second reality scenarios are destroying how our teens approach and maintain healthy friendships and romantic relationships — something they should learn during these formative years.

Equally troubling is the quantification of one's worth. Unlike the immeasurable value we place on those whom we love, social media gives everyone the privilege of ranking and scoring each other. In the past, a picture was worth a thousand words. Now, a picture is only worth the number of likes it receives. Allow me to state the obvious: Receiving a *like* on social media does not measure our worth nor does it define who we are! A *like* is simply a tap of the finger on a screen. Sometimes they are given haphazardly, sometimes carelessly, and then other times they

> THE SCREEN PROVIDES "DIGITAL COURAGE" FOR TEENS TO SAY ANYTHING WITHOUT ANY THOUGHT OF CONSEQUENCE.

are withheld maliciously.

Girls are easy prey for these games. They ask the world through social media — Am I pretty enough? Smart enough? Popular enough? Large-chested enough? Rich enough? Skinny enough? Funny enough? Their answers are based on how many *likes* they receive.

Remember my daughter's words: everyone is "searching for something to make them happy and whole. They are never satisfied."

Likes and comments aren't the only quantifiable metrics teens become disillusioned by. App makers know that in order to reach the #1 spot on iTunes or Google Play, their platform must be addictive enough to keep kids coming back day after day. Snapchat's "streak" feature is a perfect example of this. Snapchat tracks how many days you've communicated with the same person, then gives you a score everyone can see. Based on your streaks, Snapchat kindly tells you who your best friends are and whether or not those friends consider you the same. Talk about a game of jockeying for self-worth! Yet our teenagers willingly play, unaware of the thief.

This is social media for teens. They claim that they have to be on social media because "this is how we communicate now," but it is far more than just communicating. It is a search for worth, value, and validation. Every word and picture is posted in silent competition. Every tempting visual and subtle lie beckons them to forget their high worth. Once the enemy successfully garners their self-worth, he leaves FOMO, loneliness, lack of joy, jealousy, and shame in its place.

Satan is winning. He is capturing worth and leaving destruction in its wake. Since the advent of the smartphone with social media, as previously mentioned, suicide rates among young girls has increased 200 percent. Record numbers of anxiety and depression diagnoses in teens on social media are now seen by clinicians and researchers around the world.

WHAT THEY ARE REALLY ASKING FOR

Your child will ask for social media almost immediately upon receiving their first phone. To children of iGen, the smartphone *is* social media and social media *is* the smartphone.

In Matthew 7:9-11, Jesus provides a metaphor for fathers where the son is asking for bread: "Which one of you, if his son asks him for bread, will give him a stone? Or if he asks for a fish, will give him a serpent? If you then, who are evil, know how to give good gifts to your children, how much more will your Father who is in heaven give good things to those who ask him!"

In our modern society, it's pretty obvious parents know how to give good gifts to their children. Today's kids have more than someone fifty years ago could dream of having as an adult! But what if we are deceived by what is actually good? What if the gift of a new smartphone feels good and right but is really a stone in our child's hand? What if giving access to social media feels like a blessing but ends up poisoning their worth?

These are questions worth examining. Before that, let's first look at exactly what it is our children are asking for?

Foremost, they want social media, simply because this is 'what everyone does.' But what benefit or asset are they really wanting from social media?

Constant connection

Teens want the ability to keep track of friends', celebrities', and strangers' lives around the clock.

Communication

Almost every social media app has a private messaging feature that allows for online, real-time communication with anyone else using the app. These messages can be kept private from parents, who either don't know these features exist or can't see them because the teen is deleting them before they are seen. The internet-based nature of these messages makes them difficult to recover.

Freedom

They want the freedom to consume new information, create a new identity or brand, connect with whomever they want, and post their own creative content.

I believe the Matthew 7 metaphor provides an eerily clear picture of what is happening between parents and children today. Our teens are craving *bread and fish* — the good gifts of communication and connection with their peers. Parents see this as natural and healthy desires; they believe they are giving their children bread and fish. Few realize they are actually giving their children a *stone and a snake*. The stone looks like bread, but it will not sustain. Social media looks like an easy way to stay connected with friends, but it is not authentic. The snake seems innocent enough, but it is sure to bite and deliver poison to its prey. Social media looks like freedom to explore and create but it is sure to leave your child in bondage to competition and comparison.

The most common defense I hear from parents who allow social media accounts at a young age is, "I don't want my child to be left out or feel excluded from connection with their friends." Most parents would agree that feeling left out and excluded are painful emotions we hope they can avoid. But what if the same — or even worse — emotions are likely with early access to social media? What if the fear of missing out, bullying, shaming, and comparisons are worse than feeling excluded from online sharing and communication?

You must consider whether you are giving loaves of bread or heavy stones to meet your child's needs. Freedom is a beautiful gift we can give our children. Freedom to find their worth without the burden of competition and comparisons. Freedom to enhance communication skills and build deep, long-lasting friendships. Freedom to live life untethered to a device.

WHAT THEY ACTUALLY RECEIVE

Businesses use social media for advertising, non-profits use it to raise money and awareness, and schools and churches use it to connect and inform. Everyone is vying for digital attention. Despite how ubiquitous and age-independent social media has become, we have to remember it is still a tool — not a way of life. Too often, parents and teens alike don't consider how global, business-oriented, and addictive social media is.

Let's look at what our children actually receive when they gain access to social media.

Marketing

Social media is a fantastic asset for businesses' marketing teams and advertisers. When a child uses it solely for pleasure or entertainment, however, they and their data become the *products* being marketed.

The terms of service, which are rarely read and understood, allow the platforms to use, distribute, and sell anything posted as well as personal information, such as birth date, school, address, pictures, posts, likes/dislikes, location, and friends. Did you catch that? They can distribute or even sell all of your child's photos to advertising or marketing partners.[77] Instagram photos can be reused and even sold due to the flexible copyright laws.[78] Children of iGen will think this is cool as so many are hyper-focused on fame. Parents, however, must recognize that their child's picture could be used for advertising services or goods without their knowledge.

Consumerism

Through social media sites, businesses receive constant data on how to better market and sell to children based on what they post on social media.[79] Third party companies buy this information and use it to refine advertisements and drive more consumerism. While television commercials and magazine advertisements may have driven purchases in the past, this is highly personalized, targeted advertising, running as often as the app is used. Recognizing how our culture is not only more consumeristic, but also more sexualized, should lead us to question the power of influence advertisers have. At the heart of consumerism is comparison, competition, a love of money, and conforming to worldly standards, all things contrary to Godly character.

Disconnection

Teens believe they are fully connected when hundreds or thousands of 'friends' are within a few finger taps. In reality, this type of connection is often superficial. When hours and hours are spent alone with a screen, the result is often increased loneliness. The perpetual public posting and sharing of one's "story" or "highlight reel" results in perfunctory comments and likes. The truth is, when *real* life gets *real* hard, these hundreds of friends leave teens feeling more disconnected than they felt before they ever had social media. True friendship and connection happens in community — face-to-face, life-on-life community where friends cannot be un-followed or un-friended with a click.

Disordered Priorities

A teen's online platform or brand can become an all-consuming priority in his life. Life becomes about the perfect picture, the perfect hashtag, the right amount of likes, and the right amount of *chill*, so it doesn't look like they're trying *too* hard. When popularity is quantified through publicly displaying their number of friends, followers, and worth, it's not hard to see how true priorities can be neglected. The online life takes so much time to manage and maintain; there is little time left for real life experiences.

Adult Content

This is the disgusting part of social media everyone would rather pretend doesn't exist, but most certainly does. The anonymity and private nature of the internet and social networks allow for widespread distribution of sexually explicit and pornographic content. A desire for fame, popularity, or even money leads everyday teens to fill social media platforms with homemade content. A hashtag search such as #pornvideo or #sexshop on Instagram can turn up hundreds of thousands of posts. This search feature cannot be disabled. Similarly, the Discover section of

> A TEEN'S ONLINE PLATFORM OR BRAND CAN BECOME AN ALL-CONSUMING PRIORITY IN THEIR LIFE.

Snapchat provides "news" articles told through "stories" which range from *Your Oral Sex Questions Answered, Moves to Make Your Breasts Look Perkier,* and *Guys and Sex and Why They Love it.* All of this mature content rests a few taps or swipes away from the connection and communication children originally desired.

Mental Health Issues

When we mix marketing, consumerism, disconnection, disordered priorities, and adult content in young and impressionable minds, the result is mental health issues. Rates of teen depression and suicide have skyrocketed since 2011. These trends are equal among rich and poor, city and suburb, and all ethnic backgrounds.[80] In fact, Instagram and Snapchat, the current top social media platforms with teens, were reported to have the worst impact on mental health.[81]

Addiction

Many people feel smartphone and social media addiction is typical. "There aren't any harmful side effects compared to real addictive things, like cigarettes and alcohol," proponents say. The truth is that there aren't any immediate or distinctly noticeable side effects to their addictive use. Ask any teen (or adult) who regularly uses social media, and they'll likely confirm, social media's effects aren't always good.

Some teenagers have opened up about the love/hate relationship they have with their social media accounts, such as four friends who were interviewed by Nancy Jo Sales for her book *American Girls: Social Media and the Secret Lives of Teenagers.* "Social media is destroying our lives," one girl states. "So why don't you go off it?" Sales asked. "Because then we would have no life," said the girl's friend. Later in the same interview one exclaimed, "Social media causes soooooo much anxiety," while another noted, "The popularity contest — it's never been a good thing, and now that we have the actual numbers, we've become greedy. We want more attention. I think people have become obsessed with this attention. It's become an addiction to gain as much as we can. It's depressing how self-conscious we are about these things."[82] And yet, they keep using it, just like an addict. The reality is that constant connection sounds like freedom but feels a whole lot like bondage and addiction.

What if we are all deceived about what is good? Our teenagers ask for social media but, they receive from us a stone and a snake.

"Is there anyone among you who, if your child asks for bread, will give a stone?" (Matt 7:9)

DELAYED

Taking into consideration the risks and rewards, the bondage over freedom, and the feelings of worthlessness instead of esteem, the standard we will use to protect self-worth is **Delay social media access.**

This may sound like a radical concept considering the nearly universal use of social media among children with smartphones today. Many parents, although they feel apprehensive to allow it, permit social media accounts purely because they believe it is necessary for their child's social life. I heard a parent once say, "Not allowing my child to have social media would be like social suicide for them."

Is it really social suicide to delay their access to this online world of sharing? Let's look at the research and statistical data of young teens on social media. In Jean Twenge's generational analysis book, *iGen: Why Today's Super-Connected Kids Are Growing Up Less Rebellious, More Tolerant, Less Happy — and Completely Unprepared for Adulthood — and What That Means for the Rest of Us*, she imparts some hard truth about the profile and character of the iGen. What stands out predominantly is how iGen teens are less likely to go out with their friends, get their driver's license, hold jobs, read books, and do homework than any other generation past.[83] So what are teens doing these days if they aren't involved in these common activities? They are on their smartphones, of course. One great concern for ubiquitous smartphone use is that across every demographic measured, teens who spend more time on screen activities, such as social media and internet use, are more likely to be unhappy, lonely, and depressed. Conversely, teens who spend more time on non-screen activities, such as sports, reading, or hanging out with friends, are more likely to be happy and less likely to be lonely or depressed.[84] It's quite curious that parents have permitted social media on mobile screens to ensure their child's social success, yet its very use leads to emotional and mental distress.

Twenge clearly presents the growing prevalence of mental health issues among iGen teens who use social media measured across three grade levels: eighth, tenth, and twelfth grade. By and large, the youngest iGen teens were those most greatly affected. Eighth graders, usually thirteen to fourteen years old, who spend ten or more hours a week on social media were 56 percent more likely to be unhappy and were at a 27 percent increased risk for depression. Tenth graders, usually fifteen to sixteen years old, however, were only 39 percent more likely to be unhappy with heavy social media use. Interestingly, this research showed an even risk for depression with screen and non-screen activities for tenth graders. Meaning: social media use neither helped nor hurt depressive symptoms among the fifteen to sixteen year olds.[85]

Over all three grade levels, life satisfaction among iGen teens plummeted in 2015 with 31 percent more feeling lonely and 33 percent more feeling left out compared to five years earlier. What is most concerning is that all of this emotional and mental trauma can lead to suicide, especially among girls. Three times as many girls, ages twelve to fourteen, killed themselves in 2015 than in 2007[86] and a 65 percent increase in girls suicide occurred between the years 2010–2015.[87] Whether or not there is a causal link between social media use and these increased rates of depression and suicide is yet to be determined. What is currently evident is the growth of social media correlates with the growth of mental health issues.

Twenge poignantly ends her chapter on iGen's mental well-being with this: "There is a simple, free way to improve mental health. Put down the phone and do something else."[88]

If self-worth is a sense of feeling valued, having worth, and understanding purpose, then we can deduce that the best place to develop this character trait is *off* social media — most especially during the early teenage years when the risks are highest.

Delayed social media access should not be considered a restriction as much as it is an allowance. You are allowing time for the mind to develop and emotions to mature, negating some of the risk for mental health issues in the future. *Delayed social media access* ought to be viewed as a way to enable instead of hinder. You are enabling your child to experience true connection through in-person relationships. *Delayed social media* should not be considered controlling when it could, quite literally, save them from the chaos of depression, loneliness, and suicidal thoughts. There are some potential dangers in life we cannot insulate our children from, but when the evidence of mental health problems, bullying, and sexting are abundantly clear, it becomes wise to protect and delay these risks.

WHEN SOCIAL MEDIA?

Delayed doesn't mean 'never.' It simply means 'not right now.'

Delayed means until they are more resilient, less impulsive, and less at risk for mental health issues.

How long is delayed? To the age of generalized teen maturity, when they can join the work force, and drive a car: sixteen.

Practically speaking, by age sixteen, high school students should be transitioning into their final stage of full independence from Mom and Dad — driving themselves to and from their school activities, work, and hanging out with friends. Even though iGen is showing a trend towards prolonged adolescence, age sixteen is still an appropriate age to begin trusting them with adult responsibilities. A car, driver's license, and a job are all things that can build up purpose and value into one's self-worth. Perhaps this is why these sixteen-year-old tenth graders have a decreased risk for mental and emotional issues. This age group is *less* likely to feel lonely, depressed or contemplate suicide than their eighth grade counterparts.

I fully admit *Delayed social media access* is easier said than done. One reason is how non-conforming this character-building method is to teens and the world. "If all of their peers are on social media, how will my child not be completely ostracized?" is probably a question on your mind.

First, teens still connect through text. It might take a friend an extra step to text instead of sending them a snap, but when it is their only choice, they still do it.

Second, teens, especially girls, have a love/hate relationship with their social media. Sometimes, peers and friends are jealous of those who don't have social media because they live without the drama and stress it causes.

Finally, and most importantly, when a teen has no social media but wants to feel connected to her friends, she reverts back to verbal communication! They will talk, ask questions, listen to stories, and tell their own. Instead of individually absorbing or sharing stories on Instagram, friends have the chance to verbally communicate before school, in class, and during lunch. Why? Because the Instagram-less friend isn't content to sit and watch friends stare at their phones. When true connection occurs this way, the positive emotions produced reinforce the behavior to become habit.

Another question likely running through your mind is how your child will handle such a standard. Here are a few of the arguments you can prepare for:

"I need it to communicate with friends."
"I need it to work on a group project."
"I need it to keep up-to-date with what is happening in the world."
"I need to ensure people aren't talking about me behind my back."
"I want to be able to see pictures my friends post."
"My teacher told me to "Snap" a picture in order to link to my syllabus."
"I feel sheltered because I don't know what happens every day."
"I'm the only person in the entire school without it." *(My favorite!)*

With every whine, complaint, and pushback you receive because they "cannot communicate," you must think of that rock. Literally, picture an enormously heavy rock in their hands (in place of their phone) weighing their lives down. Or envision the snake slithering into their minds and asking questions like, "Are you really happy? Did that person leave you out? You seem awfully lonely. Nobody likes you. You're not as pretty as her." We must be brave and strong, remembering that we can lead them to what is good and fulfilling, instead of what weighs them down and jeopardizes their emotional health.

I am not a radical cynic of all social media; however, I am deeply concerned about how social media is changing the character and stealing the self-worth of teens. Adults are also showing trends of diminished communication in relationships as they refrain from verbally sharing details of their lives as readily, assuming it's already been seen on social media. *"What! You didn't know that? Didn't you see it on Facebook?"*

We should desire, for ourselves and our children, to use social media sensibly, with accountability, and as a supplement to in-person relationships, but never at the cost of our relationships, character, and worth.

Now, just because you are enforcing *Delayed social media access* doesn't mean your child won't get her hands on it. Whether at school or on other kids' devices, they can create secret social media accounts. Can you stop them? Not really. This is why our communication of the pros, cons, risks, and rewards is essential. We teach and inspire them to trust our boundaries. We instruct them in the way they should go. Your standard will, if nothing else, prohibit the constant use of social media on their own smartphone — assuming you've implemented the other standards discussed. If you know about the secretive use, by all means, try and put a stop to it. If you've set this standard in place — don't cave! Don't default on your commitment and "let them have it," so at least you can see what they are doing. If they are creating secret accounts now, they will continue to create secret accounts while you are watching.

The most important way to manage this standard is through communication. Talk to your child about social media as they approach age ten. Explain how global its reach is with billions from around the world logging in every day. Describe the controversy over fake and inaccurate news being spread. Teach them how social media can steal their freedom with addiction and compulsion to check and recheck for new likes, new friends, and new stories. Give details, such as some of the statistics shared in this chapter, which demonstrate how social media can diminish the quality of their relationships and communication while negatively impacting mental health.

And most importantly, talk about their worth. Not in a "you're so special and important that you deserve a medal for not even trying" kind of way. Rather in a Christ-centered way tell them, "God knew you and created you in his image. He prepared good works for you to do for His Kingdom. Jesus died for your sins so that through Him, you may have peace on this earth and everlasting life in heaven."

We must live out what we believe: our worth is found in Jesus Christ, not in the temporal and fickle world of social media.

CHAPTER EIGHT

Maintaining Sanity

We cannot always build the future for our youth,
but we can build our youth for the future.[89]

Franklin D. Roosevelt

"You've *got* to be kidding me," I exclaim as I look through the camera roll of my child's phone. "Why on earth would our child take this picture — much less leave it here for us to find???" I say in frustration to my husband.

Instantly, I feel the climate in our home change. Ryan and I brace ourselves for the storm.

Not a natural storm at least, but a storm of emotions and frustration between parent and child. As ominous as dark clouds are in a midday sky, discovering inappropriate activity on a phone or device assures a storm is near.

A close friend recently discovered her sixteen-year-old daughter was communicating with a young college-aged, youth group volunteer. By "communicating" I mean sexting, lying in order to see him, and engaging in other inappropriate behaviors. When I talked to my friend shortly after she learned all this, she could barely find her words. "I'm so frustrated! I feel angry, disrespected, deceived — ugh! When will she learn?"

The powerful winds of her storm devastated her emotions and wrecked the balance of trust between her and her daughter.

Another parent poured her exhausted heart out to me. The school called her to report that a Snapchat photo had surfaced where her son posed wearing a mask and holding a toy gun. The snap made a reference to 'shooting up the school' which quickly resulted in other students alerting authorities. "Your son," the principal said flatly, "is currently suspended and may be expelled."

Her storm came like a category five hurricane without warning. She and her husband were flooded with disbelief, frustration, fear, and a litany of other emotions.

You are probably familiar with these storms, whether you've experienced one firsthand or heard the tales from someone else. This is when a child violates a media standard or expectation. I call them storms because they can feel physically consuming, emotionally draining, and mentally exhausting — as if we are braving a storm without shelter. Also, these storms have devastating aftermaths. For some, it takes months or years to rebuild trust and self-worth.

In the storm, you feel like the worst parent in the world because your child made a bad choice and didn't exhibit the character you have worked to instill. You spend hours compiling all the details, because the internet and media keeps records. Then you walk through the emotionally taxing process of reviewing the mistakes and lessons learned with your child. You fight bitterness because *their* poor choices will cost hours of *your* time, energy, and sanity. Simultaneously, you battle fears that your child may never get it right!

I've walked through enough of these storms with my own children and with others to know that they feel the same for everyone. Whether it's an F5 tornado or a flash flood, there is a sense of dread and impending loss of sanity with each and every storm.

It's difficult to discern how much responsibility to accept as the parent who allowed the device, app, or access versus how much responsibility to assign to your child for their activity.

- Am I mad at myself for allowing that app or am I mad at my child for not making the right choice?
- Am I embarrassed because of how my child's actions reflect on me or how their actions reflect back on them?
- Shouldn't my child know better? Shouldn't I have known better?
- Do I try to "fix" the situation or let my child deal with the natural consequences and backlash?

These tough questions, like the crashing thunder of a midnight storm, will keep you awake at night. They numb your mind during the day while inflaming your emotions all evening while at home with your child. Fear of the aftermath holds you captive. You guess and second-guess the best way through the storm; yet, the wind continues to blow, and you lose your sense of direction.

These are the storms parents must brave. But, in the absence of every storm, there is calm.

MEDIA CALM

Media Calm is defined in our home as: "When all of our children know and obey the media standards we have established. Phones are put up at the right time every night, text messages are appropriate and kind, no questionable websites are visited, *and* no one complains about why they don't have more time, a newer phone, or more apps."

You're probably thinking, "Yeah right, that doesn't exist!"

I assure you, Media Calm is obtainable. We have battled fierce storms, but we spend most of our time in the calm. Every media mistake is a teachable moment, a lesson learned for all of us. Even with four teenagers and three tweens, the standard we have set, the values we reinforce, and the knowledge with which we equip them enable us to weather each storm bravely.

I acknowledge that some children won't cause any major storms. Some children are more apt to break media standards than others. Some boys' brains crave video games, and they will push time allowances in order to play. Other boys are more interested in a girl's attention and may send inappropriate text messages. Some girls tend to hypnotize themselves with the world of social media perfectionism, connection, and fame. Other girls engage in bullying over looks, fashion, or popularity. Every child is unique in their actions and impulses. There isn't one simple way to maintain sanity as you establish a level of Media Calm. However, having a media standard is foundational.

MEDIA STANDARD

Setting a media standard is the best way to maintain sanity while managing media. "What is a media standard?" you ask. It is the set of allowances and boundaries which will govern your home and the media flowing through it. This includes televisions, computers, game consoles, phones, tablets, and all the devices that are brought into your home by your child's friends. A media standard is everything we've discussed in the past seven chapters.

As you go through the following steps to create a media standard for your own family, keep in mind that the earlier you begin managing media, the easier it is. Honestly, at the pace technology grows, you almost need to decide how you'll manage media when your child is born! However, if your child is an adolescent, and you're just now getting started, you will want to consider a more comprehensive approach than if you are starting with a toddler. Furthermore, once your child has their own phone, a greater level of monitoring will be necessary. Guaranteed.

People often ask me, "How do I start over?" No matter where you are, or what you've allowed, there is always a reset button. Enlist all of your character building know-how to create a new standard for media use. I know this to be true because I have started this process on kids of varying ages. It's a bit harder to hit the reset button once they are older, but it can be done. And it's worth doing.

Step 1: Set the Standard

Ideally, you and your spouse will set the standard together, so you are in mutual agreement for how media is managed in your home. This pre-commitment will create a united front, so your child recognizes your consistency. It will also prevent future battles in your marriage. If you and your spouse are not in agreement, do the best you can to limit and restrict those areas that pose the most danger.

If you are divorced with shared custody, media standards should be agreed upon by both parents when the child spends time in both homes. I realize the difficulty in this as I have heard story after story of polarized standards between mom's house and dad's house. If an agreement cannot be reached, your standard must still be set for your home. You'll need to work harder at explaining the why to your child so they maintain your standard when not in your custody.

If you are a single parent, you must both set the standard and uphold it. You will not have anyone maintaining the standard with you; therefore, you must be realistic with how much accountability you are able to give. Remember: a standard that is set but not upheld, is only a suggestion. Create a standard you know you can achieve and hold your child accountable to. Like the divorced parent, your explanation of why should be solidly reinforced in order for the child to manage their own media when you are not able to.

Schedule a time when you will create the media standard. Ensure you are levelheaded, undistracted, and prepared to make important decisions affecting day-to-day life and your child's future. Reflect on and commit to your own media standards during this time. Remember, you must first model the behavior you wish to see. Your children will pattern themselves after you, so don't expect them to abide by standards you cannot keep yourselves.

DON'T EXPECT CHILDREN TO ABIDE BY STANDARDS YOU CANNOT KEEP YOURSELF.

Over the next few pages you will find an outline for your media standard. For additional information about creating and maintaining your media standard including up to date recommendations for third party programs and services visit:
https://managingmediabook.com/resources

SCREEN FREE AREAS

Dedicate certain areas of your home and within your lifestyle where there will be NO screens used:

- ☐ Kitchen/Dining Room
- ☐ Bedrooms
- ☐ Strollers
- ☐ Car
- ☐ Other_____

SCREEN TIME LIMITS

Establish time frames when screens are not allowed.

- ☐ One hour before bedtime
- ☐ During a meal
- ☐ In a car
- ☐ Church
- ☐ Family time
- ☐ School hours
- ☐ Other_____

Also, establish how much daily time on screens will be permitted

- ☐ Birth — eighteen months old: Zero screen time
- ☐ Eighteen months — two years old: Small amounts of co-viewed, high-quality screen use.
- ☐ Two — five years old: One hour of co-viewed high-quality programs
- ☐ Six years old and older: Two hours of safe, previewed, and age appropriate programming

Special occasions, such as long car rides or while on vacation, may dictate a variance from the day-to-day standard. A nine hour car ride to see family for the holidays may certainly dictate more screen-time. However, on the flip side of the same coin, arrival to your vacation destination is an opportune time to discontinue screen use altogether for a week.

SCREEN TIME ALLOWANCES

What type of digital media will your child be allowed to engage with?

- Internet browsing
    - o   On what devices (computer, Xbox, smart TV, tablet)
    - o   Specific websites allowed
    - o   Specific websites to be blocked
    - o   Categories of websites to be blocked

- Games
    - o   On what devices (console, computer, handheld, device, phone)
    - o   What rating? (i.e. E for Everyone or 4+ in app store)
    - o   Single or multiplayer?
    - o   What types? (MMORPG, first person shooter, strategy, sports)
    - o   Allows online messaging or adding friends?

- Television/Movies/Netflix
    - o   On what device (television, computer, tablet, phone)
    - o   What type of programming?
    - o   Ratings?

- Social Media
    - o   Sixteen years old
    - o   Which platform? We recommend no more than one!

PRE-VIEWING, CO-VIEWING, & CO-PLAYING

As the media industry produces more internet-ready toys, graphically realistic video games, and controversial movies, the need for parents' presence is greater than ever.

For younger children, you should research or pre-view a new game, show, or website they wish to access. Checking age-level limits for appropriateness, as well as for any potential advertisements is vital for their protection and innocence. Often times, gaming apps' content is fine but the advertisement pop-ups can be shockingly inappropriate.

Another option, especially good for older adolescents and teenagers, is to co-view or co-play new media with them. Whether they are searching online for homework or a YouTube video, watching a Netflix original series, or playing a newly downloaded game on PlayStation, your active presence at the start can help them understand and interpret any difficult content.

THE BOTTOM LINE IS THAT YOU SHOULD KNOW WHAT MEDIA IS STREAMING INTO YOUR HOME.

The bottom line is that you should know what media is streaming into your home. If you've never heard of it, you must educate yourself.

And if your research leaves questions, you must pre-view, co-view, or co-play — or be brave, and say no.

PARENTAL CONTROLS

Nearly all devices allow for parental controls. These are the best way to secure boundaries when not co-viewing or co-playing with your child. These controls allow for everything from disabling the web browser to time limits.

☐ Computers
☐ Tablets
☐ E-Readers
☐ Smartphones
☐ Smart TVs
☐ Video game consoles
☐ Smart watches

SMARTPHONES

Smartphones open up a new world of freedom for children. You must intentionally decide what type of smart features will be accessible to your child as they carry the device.

☐ Internet
☐ Camera
☐ Facetime/Video Chat
☐ Games
☐ Productivity apps
☐ MMS
☐ Texting and texting apps
☐ Social media
☐ App store access
☐ Music
☐ Videos/Movies

As you have learned, children should *Wait for the privilege* of having all of these smart phone features. As you set the smartphone standard, consider how and when your child can earn more privileges.

This is only a basic outline for you to create a media standard for your home. All of these media types will require a decision at one point or another. Some items may require compromise from one spouse, but ultimately you both must be reading from the same rule book when you are finished. Sanity is so much easier when you are in full agreement.

Step 2: Establish Consequences

After you've hashed out your standard, you must decide on appropriate, logical consequences for when the media standard's boundaries are broken. These are best decided in advance rather than during the storm or even in its aftermath. Some things may only require a conversation and redirection, while others may require the loss of the privilege for a period of time.

For younger children, establish screen-time as a privilege, not as a norm. This can be accomplished easily through checklists of what must be done to earn the privilege. For example:

Before you play on tablet, watch TV, or play video games, have you done this?

- ✓ *Finished your daily chores*
- ✓ *Cleaned your room*
- ✓ *Read a book for 30 minutes*
- ✓ *Completed all homework*
- ✓ *Taken the dog on a walk*
- ✓ *Played outside for 1 hour*

Here, the consequence for not accomplishing daily tasks is a loss of screen-time. This helps build their character as they learn responsibility, prioritizing, and delayed gratification. You'll need to decide exactly what earns the privilege of screen-time. The key lessons with young children will be through continual, open discussions about how character can be displayed with the technology they enjoy. Additionally, praise them when they demonstrate good character.

Your presence, role-modeling, and guidance for young children should prevent the need for any punishments regarding how they engage with screens and media. If you have parental controls set up on your devices, they will protect them from straying outside your boundaries. However, if a child throws a device across the room in anger and shatters the screen, you may want to consider a greater consequence than loss of screen-time.

Tweens and teens with a smartphone or device, on the other hand, require a different approach. Teens operate best when the expectations are known. Their rapid brain growth leads to forgetfulness; therefore, a written contract may be beneficial for teenagers who have greater privileges and need clearly defined consequences for major infractions. For example:

> "In order to maintain the privilege of using Instagram, I agree not to post any selfies, not to follow people I don't know, only to allow people I know to follow me, and not to 'like' any content that would degrade my integrity and character.
>
> If I break this agreement, I understand the consequence is the app will be deleted from my phone for one month. If I break this agreement again, I understand that the Instagram app will be removed from my phone for six months."

It may seem like a daunting task to pre-commit to consequences for the innumerous things that could break the media standard. Choose the big items that affect character first: disrespectful conduct, unkind communication, deleting content, inappropriate pictures, and social media use/misuse. Similar to the example above, detail exactly what the consequence will be if the standard is broken.

Another important area of consequence for teens is where and how much the phone or device is used. For example, if you choose not to allow its use behind closed doors, you will need to establish a consequence if this is not followed. Likewise, if you set a standard for the phone or device not to be checked or used out of boredom (a standard I highly recommend), what will the consequence be if they are looking down at the screen every free second?

The idea isn't to become horrifically legalistic about every possible consequence. Healthy media standards and behavior do not come easy though. The allure and pleasure of screens makes them extremely difficult to resist, and the only way to withstand the temptation is with a set standard of practice. The more the standard is upheld and honored; the more natural and uncomplicated it will become.

Step 3: Write it out

Plain and simple: you will forget parts of your standard if it is not recorded. Therefore, write out the standard and consequences you've established in Steps 1 and 2. This will serve as your roadmap — a set of directions to guide you, especially when you've lost all sense of direction amidst a blinding storm. Your written standard will be your compass directing you exactly where to go when emotions and fears are heightened in a storm.

Consider how frustrating it is to fight over directions with your spouse, or any companion for that matter, on a road trip. The same is true here. You need to map out your agreed course in advance and not waiver at the crossroads. If needed, you can reevaluate your roadmap together during Media Calm, but in the storm, you follow the route you have already agreed upon.

Also, your likeliness to forget is rivaled by your child's memory. If they can get away without an enforced consequence, they will. Rarely will a child remind a parent, "Don't forget, I'm grounded from my iPad today!" No way. Children learn best in clearly defined and *kept* boundaries. If the boundary is established but never kept, it's really not a boundary at all, and the child knows it.

Step 4: Communicate

After you have everything documented, you must verbally communicate your established media standard with your children. You will most likely have their full attention, because they tend to highly value their screen and media time.

Ultimately, you must describe why God desires a higher character. Talk it through to see if they can recognize unfavorable character in other people or if they have seen how media and technology can corrupt good character. *Remember, you have been the role model, so brace yourself for the possible answer!* Express how these boundaries and standards will work to build their character — and yours! Children desire to understand, so use whatever means necessary to help them grasp why patience is important, how self-control will benefit them, and why God desires these character traits.

Your aim is not to solely read a list of 'do this and do not do this'. Rather, explain *why* you are establishing this media standard with these boundaries. Explain what their media *privileges* are instead of what media *limitations* they have. When children know the *why*, they are more likely to act according to your *how*.

Be a good listener during this time. If there is space for compromise on some privileges, this gives your child the opportunity to demonstrate respect, negotiation, and communication skills. Depending on their age, compromise can be imperative for their cooperation with your standard. Your child will feel valued for being heard and having an active part in this process.

Explaining the privilege is more empowering than stating the consequences. This keeps the focus on character building through the screen's use. You can say something like this:

> "You may download one new game app per week, which can be added on Saturdays. You'll need to practice your patience and self-control skills during the week in order to earn this privilege."

This type of verbal boundary directive works great for young children and adolescents. If the child asks repeatedly during the week for a new app, you remind them about patience and self-control. If or when they earn the privilege, praise them for exhibiting the excellent character of patience in waiting, respect for this standard, and self-control for not asking throughout the week.

As I mentioned in Step 2, a written contract of sorts may be beneficial for older children with more privileges and more opportunities to blow past boundaries. The standard and established consequences must be communicated with your child and mutually agreed upon. This gives them the freedom to demonstrate responsibility and trust within the boundaries in order to earn wider boundaries or more privileges.

In the future, if they choose not to operate within the standard's boundaries, but they have agreed to the consequences, emotions inside the storm will not alter the consequence. The parent and child can easily refer back to the roadmap, or contract, to know what was agreed upon. This keeps the consequence fair and consistent.

For every week, month, or year that goes by when the standard is not broken, give them praise and widen their boundaries. Let them know you are proud of their respect for the rules, self-control, humility, and self-worth. Be sure they know their good character is seen and valued.

These four steps: Set the standard, Establish consequences, Write it out, and Communicate help you practically establish a media standard in your home. Building this standard will prove futile, however, if it is not built on a solid foundation.

FOUNDATION

One day Jesus said to his disciples, "Let's cross to the other side of the lake." So they got into a boat and started out.

As they sailed across, Jesus settled down for a nap. But soon a fierce storm came down on the lake. The boat was filling with water, and they were in real danger.

The disciples went and woke him up, shouting, "Master, Master, we're going to drown!" When Jesus woke up, he rebuked the wind and the raging waves. Suddenly the storm stopped and all was calm. Then he asked them, "Where is your faith?"

The disciples were terrified and amazed. "Who is this man?" they asked each other. "When he gives a command, even the wind and waves obey him!"

Luke 8:22-25

The disciples were enjoying the calm, peace, and rest of Jesus' presence. They obeyed His directives and trusted His guidance. Even still, a fierce storm came upon them. A storm so dangerous, they feared for their lives.

In their helplessness and despair, they cried out to Jesus, awakening him. The wind and waves respond immediately to Jesus' rebuke, and all was calm once again. The disciples who feared the storm were now in reverence, awe, and holy fear of the Son of God.

We cannot attempt to maintain sanity without the One whom the wind and waves obey. When a storm hits our home, we must act as the disciples did: cry out for Jesus. He can quiet our fears as easily as he silences the wind. He can rebuke the waves and create calm. We should not expect Him to immediately rebuke the storm and create calm, although He can and delights in doing so. Rather, in faith, we must seek to see His glory revealed through the storm. Jesus demonstrated his glory to his disciples, and He wants to do the same for us. Each and every storm can teach us a lesson, grow our faith, and bring God glory.

> **WE CANNOT ATTEMPT TO MAINTAIN SANITY WITHOUT THE ONE WHOM THE WIND AND WAVES OBEY.**

Yes, Jesus is the foundation, but your trust in Him does not exempt you from acting on what you now know. If you've read up to this point, any media ignorance you once had is gone. By now you know to respect the power of technology, the dangers of limitless access, to be alert for the enemy's schemes, and how easily your child's character can be reshaped by addictive media.

When there is moral rot within a nation, its government topples easily. But wise and knowledgeable leaders bring stability.

Proverbs 28:2 (NLT)

With the knowledge you've gained, you must wisely lead your family. Together, as brave parents, we can reestablish a holy standard for living and raising children in the digital age. We are not called to conform to this world. We are to be transformed by renewing our minds (Rom 12:2). This renewing is the shifting of the qualities of our character back into alignment with the Word of God.

Smartphones, internet, video games — God allowed the creation of it all, but this doesn't mean we lose sight of who God intended us to be. Our standards will lead to a transformation. Our path will no longer be an uncharted, rocky terrain, but a paved road with a firm foundation for others to follow.

EPILOGUE

It was the last week of school and I was driving one of my daughters, age fifteen at the time, to school along with her friend. I half listened to them gabbing while my mind shuffled through all of my to-do, to-make, to-clean, to-email, to-wash, and to-ask lists like a well-worn deck of cards. My tried and true method for making sure I don't forget something with each of my children proved beneficial on this day.

"Hey," I called to my daughter looking back through the rear view mirror, "did you call the donut shop back yet? Didn't you say they called yesterday and left a message?"

"Oh yeah! I better call them right now." Without hesitation she found the number in her call history and called back.

She had just applied for a summer job at a local, family-owned donut shop. While only fifteen, she had hopes she could still get hired on for the summer. It was only a five minute drive from our house, and working early morning hours was an ideal first job for her.

"Hi, my name is...." She started the conversation strong. "I received a voicemail yesterday about the application I turned in for a job and I'm returning the call."

"Yes, ma'am." I heard her repeat politely in response to the employer on the other end. "I can come in anytime on Friday morning. 11 am? Yes ma'am I will see you at 11 am Friday morning."

As she ended the call, her friend, sharing the back seat with her, stared in awe. Closing her jaw, she managed to say, "I cannot even believe you just picked up the phone and called someone like that. I could never have done that."

I met my daughter's eye as we stopped at a stop sign. "I'm proud of you. Way to jump on that task and get it done. You were very respectful."

She looked at her friend, "What's the big deal about calling someone?"

Come that Friday morning, my daughter was offered the job after a short interview. After a mini celebration in the car, I asked for more details. She began, "The manager enjoyed how personable and outgoing I was. She said it was important for customer service."

When I heard my daughter say this, my heart swelled and I immediately recognized two things. First, my daughter's ability to verbally communicate was far superior compared to her peers and it shined through in her interview. Second, the Lord was blessing her good character.

I briefly mentioned to her why I believed her communication skills were so good: We don't allow her to spend all day communicating through her phone and social media. I followed up with praise to God for his favor and blessing through this job.

"Yeah, maybe…," she deflected, like a true teenager.

Two months later, my working-six-days-a-week daughter caught wind of a white Ford Mustang for sale in the neighborhood next to ours. She fiercely desired this car. After two months of working, she was concerned that someone else might buy the Mustang before she could. She boldly walked to the home with the Mustang and rang the doorbell.

"Hi, my name is......I live in the next neighborhood. I'm here to ask about the Ford Mustang you have for sale in your driveway." She got the conversation rolling as she stood on his front step intentionally wearing her Donut Shop work t-shirt.

"It says $5,000 firm, but I was wondering if you would take less. I'm fifteen years old and have been working all summer — everyday but Sundays and starting early in the morning — but I still don't have enough." My girl was seriously working her negotiating skills. I believe it may have also been mentioned that she is one of seven adopted children.

The very next day, my husband and daughter walked to this man's house and paid $4,000 for my daughter's first car: a beautiful, used 2008 Ford Mustang.

Now, lest you chastise us for allowing a "sports car" as her first car, let's focus on the fruit of this story.

My iGen daughter, who has had strict phone and media standards for all of her adolescent and teenager years, demonstrated more adult-like competency skills than many millennial adults I've met. She displayed patience through getting a job, working hard, and saving her money. She showed respect to everyone, including herself. She was kind and honest in all her dealings. Self-control was demonstrated throughout as she saved her money. Once she owned her Mustang, her inaccessibility to social media and inability to send pictures kept her humble. Instead of posting boastful pictures sure to make others feel 'less than', she shared the story with her friends over texts and phone calls. And finally, her self-worth was affirmed by her boss, thankful for having such a hard worker; from the man selling his car, impressed by a fifteen-year-old's confidence and ability to take such initiative; and from us, her parents, proud of the young woman she was becoming.

All of the character trait seeds we planted, nurtured, watered, prayed for, and fought for were now producing abundant fruit! And not only was she benefiting from this fantastic fruit, others were as well. Her coworkers and customers at the donut shop, teachers, coaches, friends, siblings, and parents were all blessed through her blooming and beautiful character.

FRUIT

This story isn't the end all, be all. None of my children or us are beyond reproach. We are very much still learning, planting, nurturing, watering, praying for, and fighting for those character traits to bloom in other areas of all our children's lives. It is a continual process, much like gardening.

Of the many hats I wear, gardener is not one of them. I don't claim to know gardening, but I do understand its concepts, and it is the perfect parallel to parenting and discipling children.

One key to gardening is to feed the soil, not the plant. This is a fantastic analogy for parenting children because as the soil holds the seed, the heart holds our child's character. You could modify this gardening rule to apply to our character-building standard: feed the heart, not the flesh.

The plant is the visible portion of the growing seed. It may appear desperate for water and nourishment to survive, but watering the leaves will do nothing to nourish the plant. At the end of the day, all of its strength to grow comes from its roots in the soil.

In the same way, our child's behavior and desire for screens and media is what is seen. It may appear that we must satisfy these desires in order for them to thrive or even survive, but this does not produce fruit! It is the heart that produces fruitful character when it is fed and cultivated. Giving in to our children's media desires is like watering the leaves of a plant.

It has been said, "The best fertilizer is the shadow of the gardener." As a parent committed to cultivating a heart of Godly character, the best supplement we can give our children's growth is our shadow. This is not a shadow which hovers and solves their problems for them. Our shadow is our supervision and guidance over this potentially dangerous and addictive area of life. We can protect them from media-induced damage, shame, sin, and regret when we define and maintain a standard of character.

Also, if a gardener knew his crop could be eaten up by deer, wouldn't he do something to prevent this? Maybe he'd erect a fence or some type of boundary for the crop's protection. Parents, much like a gardener, must be present, watchful, and willing to set up boundaries to cultivate healthy growth and abundant fruit.

A gardener cannot plant seeds, ignore them for six months, and then return expecting abundant fruit. In the same way, parents cannot ask children to behave online, ignore their activity for months, and then check in expecting to see character and competency.

OUR HARD VS THEIR HARD

Life would be so much easier if we just gave our children what they wanted. If meeting their every desire the moment they proclaimed it actually made for more competent adults, we wouldn't be grappling with the problems we face today.

But parenting is not that easy. In fact, it's not easy at all in our current times.

Unlike when we grew up, when natural consequences taught us the majority of our lessons, the natural consequences of media misuse today comes at a very high cost. From shame, regret, and loss of opportunity all the way to death, these natural consequences can cause pain and harm that isn't easily undone or forgotten.

In contrast to natural consequences are logical consequences. These are imposed by a parent, teacher, or other authority figure. These are what you established as you created your media standard in Chapter 8. They are different from punishments, as logical consequences are decided upon in advance, often planned with a child's knowledge, and make sense in relation to the behavior.

Parents have the ability to choose which type of consequences their children will learn by. Both can have advantages, but one is always harder than the other. As the parent, following through on media-related, logical consequences is time-consuming and exhausting. On the other hand, allowing children to face natural consequences requires very little effort of our own. For children, media-related, logical consequences are at worst, annoying. A child's natural consequences, however, can be life-altering — leading to depression, anxiety, and suicide. Many of these natural consequences are piggy-backed with legal consequences.

This is where we must choose: *our hard* versus *their hard*.

Our hard, enforcing logical consequences or *their hard*, living with the permanent repercussions of media misuse.

As I struggle to bond and form relationships with older adopted children, I often want to give my kids everything that will make them happy and — if I'm honest — make them like me. I grow weak and want to rationalize, *my kids just want to fit in with all of their peers....they've been through enough hard stuff.* I can begin to question all of this long term character stuff.

But my husband and I committed ourselves to a standard of character development. Allowing our children to fit in with peers does not exempt them from hard consequences, nor does trying to make their life easy so they are happy. Neither of us *enjoy* the arduous work of maintaining boundaries and logical consequences with a house full of children. We delay our gratification, knowing this is temporary, and look toward their future character.

Our temporary hard is a lot easier than their lifelong hard.

We must do the hard, brave work. We point to our Savior, Jesus Christ, model the behavior we desire to see, set up healthy boundaries, build character through our relationships, and delay gratification.

And then, we may enjoy the sweet fruits of our hard labor: competent adults with God-honoring character and integrity, bravely raising our grandchildren to have the character God desires.

Be strong and brave. Get to work.
Don't be afraid. Don't lose hope…

1 Chr 28:20 (NIRV)

This is so that the next generation and
children not yet born will know these
things, and so they can rise up and tell
their children.

Psalm 78:6 (CEB)

ABOUT THE AUTHOR

Kelly Newcom is the founder of Brave Parenting, an organization that empowers and equips parents to do the brave work of raising children of character amidst a culture of instant and limitless gratification. Although she holds a pharmacy degree from Purdue University and continues to practice community pharmacy part-time, Kelly is most passionate to reach parents around the globe with the message of 'character over media.' She loves Jesus, coffee, and community.

Kelly and her husband, Ryan, have been married for sixteen years and have seven foster-adopted children, four boys and three girls, ages ten to nineteen. When not cheering one another on at sporting events or concerts, she and her family love drive-in movies, board games, and the beach. They live just outside of San Antonio, Texas.

ABOUT BRAVE PARENTING

Brave Parenting is an organization empowering and equipping parents to do the brave, hard work of raising children of character and integrity in a culture of instant and limitless gratification. Their goal is to (re)shape the next generation for the glory and kingdom of God by focusing on character over media, comfort, and culture.

Founded in 2015 out of obedience to the calling to speak out on the topic of kids and media, namely smartphones. Today, they educate schools, churches, and parent groups on creating media standards and to bravely fight the good fight for the character God desires.

For booking inquiries visit https://braveparenting.net

DEFINING EACH GENERATION

Baby Boomers: Those born in the years 1946-1964

Generation X: Those born in the years 1965-1979

Millennial: Those born in the years 1980-1995
Sometime referred to as Generation Y

iGen: Estimated as those born in the years 1995-2012.
Sometimes referred to as Generation Z

COMMON TEXTING ACRONYMS

8	Oral Sex	**AF**	As F**K
143	I Love You	**BRB**	Be Right Back
ILY	I Love You	**BTW**	By The Way
CU46	See You For Sex	**DBEYR**	Don't Believe Everything You Read
GNOC	Get Naked On Cam	**FWIW**	For What It's Worth
GNRN	Get Naked Right Now	**GR8**	Great
IWS	I Want Sex	**IMHO**	In My Humble Opinion
S2R	Send To Receive	**IRL**	In Real Life
SORG	Straight OR Gay	**ISO**	In Search Of
PAW	Parents Are Watching	**LMAO**	Laughing My A** Off
PIR	Parent In Room	**POV**	Point Of View
POS	Parent Over Shoulder	**RBTL**	Read Between The Lines
YWS	You Want Sex	**STBY**	Sucks To Be You
WYCM	Will You Call Me	**WTF**	What The F**K
CD9/ CODE 9	Parent/Adult Around	**WYWH**	Wish You Were Here

NOTES

[1] Positions and Functions of the Four Brain Lobes. (n.d.). Retrieved from MD Health: http://www.md-health.com/Lobes-Of-The-Brain.html

[2] Edmonds, M. (n.d.). Are Teenage Brains Really Different From Adult Brains? Retrieved from How Stuff Works: http://science.howstuffworks.com/life/inside-the-mind/human-brain/teenage-brain1.htm

[3] Hunt, E. (2015, November 3). Essena O'Neill quits Instagram claiming social media 'is not real life'. Retrieved from The Guardian: https://www.theguardian.com/media/2015/nov/03/instagram-star-essena-oneill-quits-2d-life-to-reveal-true-story-behind-images

[4] O'Neill, E. (n.d.). I Open at the Close. Retrieved from Tumblr: http://agirlnamedally.tumblr.com/post/136577427665/hello-can-anyone-please-make-this-email-from

[5] Heraclitus. (n.d.). Heraclitus Quotes. Retrieved from Brainy Quotes: https://www.brainyquote.com/quotes/authors/h/heraclitus.html

[6] Dalrymple, J. (2011, April 28). The Truth About Android vs. iPhone Market Share. Retrieved from The Loop: http://www.loopinsight.com/2011/04/28/the-truth-about-android-vs-iphone-market-share/

[7] Smith, A. (2011, July 11). Smartphone Adoption and Usage. Retrieved from Pew Research Center: http://www.pewinternet.org/2011/07/11/smartphone-adoption-and-usage/

[8] Lenhart, A. (2012, March 19). Teens, Smartphones, & Texting. Retrieved from Pew Research Center: http://www.pewinternet.org/2012/03/19/teens-smartphones-texting/

[9] Silver, K., & Clodfelter, K. (n.d.). Best Baby Apps. Retrieved from Parents: http://www.parents.com/fun/entertainment/gadgets/best-iphone-apps-for-baby/

[10] Kardaras, N. (2016, August 27). It's 'digital heroin': How screens turn kids into psychotic junkies. Retrieved from New York Post: http://nypost.com/2016/08/27/its-digital-heroin-how-screens-turn-kids-into-psychotic-junkies/

[11] Victoria L. Dunckley, M. (2015). Reset Your Child's Brain. Novato: New World Library.

[12] Victoria L. Dunckley, M. (2015). Reset Your Child's Brain. Novato: New World Library.

[13] Definition of Need. (n.d.). Retrieved from Dictionary.com: http://www.dictionary.com/browse/need?s=t

[14] Grunwald Associates LLC. (2013). Living and Learning with Mobile Devices: What Parents Think About Mobile Devices for Early Childhood and K-12 Learning. Retrieved from http://www.grunwald.com/pdfs/Grunwald%20Mobile%20Study%20public%20report.pdf

[15] Radesky, J., & Christakis, D. (2016, November). Media and Young Minds: Council on Communications and Media. Retrieved from American Academy of Pediatrics News and Journals Gateway: http://pediatrics.aappublications.org/content/138/5/e20162591

[16] Misra, S., Cheng, L., Genevie, J., & Yuan, M. (2014). The iPhone Effect: The quality of in-person social interactions in the presence of mobile device. Environment & Behavior, 1-24.

[17] Turkle, S. (2015, September 26). Stop Googling. Let's Talk. Retrieved from New York Times: https://www.nytimes.com/2015/09/27/opinion/sunday/stop-googling-lets-talk.html

[18] Ward, A. F., Duke, K., Gneezy, A., & Bos, M. W. (2017, April 3). Brain Drain: The Mere Presence of One's Own Smartphone Reduces Available Cognitive Capacity. Retrieved from The University of Chicago Press Journals: http://www.journals.uchicago.edu/doi/abs/10.1086/691462

[19] Turkle, S. (2015, September 26). Stop Googling. Let's Talk. Retrieved from New York Times: https://www.nytimes.com/2015/09/27/opinion/sunday/stop-googling-lets-talk.html

[20] Boudette, N. E. (2016, November 15). Biggest Spike in Traffic Deaths in 50 years? Blame Apps. Retrieved from New York Times: https://www.nytimes.com/2016/11/16/business/tech-distractions-blamed-for-rise-in-traffic-fatalities.html

[21] Christensen, M. A., Bettencourt, L., Kaye, L., Moturu, S. T., Nguyen, K. T., Olgin, J. E., . . . Marcus, G. M. (2016, November 9). Direct Measuremens of

Smartphone Screen-Time: Relationships with Demographics and Sleep. Retrieved from PLOS: http://journals.plos.org/plosone/article?id=10.1371/journal.pone.0165331

[22] Hunley, S. (2017, March 3). Problematic Smartphone Use and Its Relationship to Anxiety and Depression. Retrieved from Anxiety.org: https://www.anxiety.org/smartphone-use-and-its-relationship-to-anxiety-and-depression

[23] Perry, L. D. (2016, June). Impact of Pornography on Children. Retrieved from American College of Pediatricians: https://www.acpeds.org/the-college-speaks/position-statements/the-impact-of-pornography-on-children

[24] Ehmke, R. (n.d.). How Using Social Media Affects Teenagers. Retrieved from Child Mind Institute: https://childmind.org/article/how-using-social-media-affects-teenagers/

[25] Richtel, M. (2017, March 13). Are Teenagers Replacing Drugs with Smartphones? Retrieved from New York Times: https://www.nytimes.com/2017/03/13/health/teenagers-drugs-smartphones.html

[26] Ward, A. F., Duke, K., Gneezy, A., & Bos, M. W. (2017, April 3). Brain Drain: The Mere Presence of One's Own Smartphone Reduces Available Cognitive Capacity. Retrieved from The University of Chicago Press Journals: http://www.journals.uchicago.edu/doi/abs/10.1086/691462

[27] Kid & Tech: The Evolution of Today's Digital Natives. (n.d.). Retrieved from Influence Central: http://influence-central.com/kids-tech-the-evolution-of-todays-digital-natives/

[28] Lenhart, A. (2012, March 19). Teens, Smartphones & Texting. Retrieved from Pew Research Center: http://www.pewinternet.org/2012/03/19/teens-smartphones-texting/

[29] Radesky, J., & Christakis, D. (2016, November). Media and Young Minds: Council on Communications and Media. Retrieved from American Academy of Pediatrics News and Journals Gateway: http://pediatrics.aappublications.org/content/138/5/e20162591

[30] 25 Surprising Facts About Phone Addiction. (2015, February 22). Retrieved from Addiction Tips: http://www.addictiontips.net/phone-addiction/phone-addiction-facts/

[31] Abraham Lincoln quotes. (n.d.). Retrieved from Brainy Quotes: https://www.brainyquote.com/quotes/authors/a/abraham_lincoln.html

[32] Definition of respect. (n.d.). Retrieved from English Oxford Living Dictionaries: https://en.oxforddictionaries.com/definition/respect

[33] Definition of respect. (n.d.). Retrieved from Merriam-Webster: https://www.merriam-webster.com/dictionary/respect

[34] Mann, C. (2012, January 6). Is Dakota Fanning too young for her Cosmo cover? Retrieved from CBS News: https://www.cbsnews.com/news/is-dakota-fanning-too-young-for-her-cosmo-cover/

[35] Gibson, K. (2017, January 8). Hilary Duff on Coparenting With Ex Mike Comrie: "I Wouldn't Choose Anyone Else". Retrieved from Popsugar: https://www.popsugar.com/celebrity/Hilary-Duff-Cosmopolitan-February-Issue-2017-42940750

[36] For Most Smartphone Users, It's Round-the-Clock Connection. (2017, January 26). Retrieved from Report Linker: https://www.reportlinker.com/insight/smartphone-connection.html

[37] Mark Twain quotes. (n.d.). Retrieved from Brainy Quotes: https://www.brainyquote.com/search_results.html?q=mark+twain

[38] U.S. Department of Health and Human Services. (n.d.). Bullying Definition. Retrieved from Stop Bullying.gov: https://www.stopbullying.gov/what-is-bullying/definition/index.html

[39] Online Shaming. (n.d.). Retrieved from Wikipedia: https://en.wikipedia.org/wiki/Online_shaming

[40] The Top Six Unforgettable CyberBullying Cases Ever. (2013, April 23). Retrieved from No Bullying.com: https://nobullying.com/six-unforgettable-cyber-bullying-cases/

[41] The Top Six Unforgettable CyberBullying Cases Ever. (2013, April 23). Retrieved from No Bullying.com: https://nobullying.com/six-unforgettable-cyber-bullying-cases/

[42] The Top Six Unforgettable CyberBullying Cases Ever. (2013, April 23). Retrieved from No Bullying.com: https://nobullying.com/six-unforgettable-cyber-bullying-cases/

[43] The Top Six Unforgettable CyberBullying Cases Ever. (2013, April 23).

Retrieved from No Bullying.com: https://nobullying.com/six-unforgettable-cyber-bullying-cases/

44 Sanchez, R., & Lance, N. (2017, June 17). Judge finds Michelle Carter guilty of manslaughter in texting suicide case. Retrieved from CNN: http://www.cnn.com/2017/06/16/us/michelle-carter-texting-case/index.html

45 Williams, C. (2017, April 7). Michigan boy, 11, hangs himself after social media prank; juvenile charged. Retrieved from Chicago Tribune: http://www.chicagotribune.com/news/nationworld/midwest/ct-suicide-social-media-prank-20170407-story.html

46 Brown, R. C., & Plener, P. L. (2017, March 17). Non-Suicidal Self Injury in Adolesence. Retrieved from US National Library of Medicine Current Psychiatric Reports: https://www.ncbi.nlm.nih.gov/pmc/articles/PMC5357256/

47 Twenge, J.M., Joiner, T.E., & Rogers, M.L. (2017). Increases in Depressive Symptoms, Suicide-Related Outcomes, and Suicide Rates Among U.S. Adolescents After 2010 and Links to Increased New Media Screen Time. *Clinical Psychological Science*, 6.

48 Fox-Brewster, T. (2017, August 3). This $1 Billion App Can't 'Kik" Its Huge Child Exploitation Problem. Retrieved from Forbes: https://www.forbes.com/sites/thomasbrewster/2017/08/03/kik-has-a-massive-child-abuse-problem/#706e438d1a14

49 Kardaras, N. (2016, August 27). It's 'digital heroin': How screens turn kids into psychotic junkies. Retrieved from New York Post: http://nypost.com/2016/08/27/its-digital-heroin-how-screens-turn-kids-into-psychotic-junkies/

50 James E. Faust Quotes. (n.d.). Retrieved from Brainy Quotes: https://www.brainyquote.com/quotes/authors/j/james_e_faust.html

51 Shearer, E., & Gottfried, J. (2017, September 7). News Use Across Social Media Platforms 2017. Retrieved from Pew Research Center`: http://www.journalism.org/2017/09/07/news-use-across-social-media-platforms-2017/

52 How confident are you that you can tell real from fake news? (2017, August). Retrieved from Statista: https://www.statista.com/statistics/657090/fake-news-recogition-confidence/

53 Screen Definition. (n.d.). Retrieved from Dictionary.com:

http://www.dictionary.com/browse/screen?s=t

[54] Alter, C. (2016, April 22). U.S. Suicide Rate Rises Precipitiously, Especially Among Women. Retrieved from Time Health: http://time.com/4304621/suicide-rate-cdc-women

[55] Fox-Brewster, T. (2017, August 3). This $1 Billion App Can't 'Kik" Its Huge Child Exploitation Problem. Retrieved from Forbes: https://www.forbes.com/sites/thomasbrewster/2017/08/03/kik-has-a-massive-child-abuse-problem/#706e438d1a14

[56] Benjamin Franklin quotes. (n.d.). Retrieved from Quotes: http://www.quotes.net/quote/3914

[57] Baumeister, R. F., Bratslavsky, E., Muraven, M., & Tice, D. M. (1998). Ego Depletion: Is the Active Self a Limited Resource? Retrieved from http://faculty.washington.edu/jdb/345/345%20Articles/Baumeister%20et%20al.%20%281998%29.pdf

[58] Napoleon Bonaparte Quote. (n.d.). Retrieved from IZQuotes: http://izquotes.com/quote/378480

[59] Lewak, D. (2017, August 5). The Shocking, scandolous marriage of Robert and Kris Kardashian. Retrieved from Page Six: http://pagesix.com/2017/08/05/the-sordid-kardashian-family-history-you-dont-know-about/

[60] Best Sellers: Hardcover Advice and Misc. (2011, January 2). Retrieved from New York Times: https://www.nytimes.com/books/best-sellers/2011/01/02/hardcover-advice/

[61] Best Sellers: Celebrities. (2015, June). Retrieved from New York Times: https://www.nytimes.com/books/best-sellers/2015/06/14/celebrities/?mcubz=1

[62] Kim Kardashian Selfish. (2015, May 5). Retrieved from Amazon.com: https://www.amazon.com/Kim-Kardashian-Selfish-West/dp/0789329204/ref=pd_sim_14_3?_encoding=UTF8&pd_rd_i=0789329204&pd_rd_r=QSYTSDZTXHPW9HDB9218&pd_rd_w=wwpsk&pd_rd_wg=LPvQT&psc=1&refRID=QSYTSDZTXHPW9HDB9218

[63] 11 of the Most Ridiculous Things Kim Kardashian Has Ever Said. (2014, July 21). Retrieved from Life & Style Magazine: http://www.lifeandstylemag.com/posts/11-of-the-most-ridiculous-things-kim-

kardashian-has-ever-said-40706/photos/kim-kardashian-instagram-selfie-47827#photo-anchor

[64] Kim Kardashian Just Did a Nude Instagram Photoshoot (Again). (2016, June 2). Retrieved from Harpers Bazaar: Erica Gonzales

[65] Women spend five hours a week taking selfies. (2015, April 24). Retrieved from Daily Mail.com: http://www.dailymail.co.uk/femail/article-3053822/Women-spend-FIVE-HOURS-week-taking-selfies-one-five-upload-social-media-make-ex-partner-jealous.html

[66] Hale, K. (2017, May 25). Is Teenage Plastic Surgery a Feminist Act. Retrieved from Harpers Bazaar: http://www.harpersbazaar.com/culture/features/a9555312/teenage-plastic-surgery-feminism/

[67] Surgeons, A. S. (2016). 2016 Plastic Surgery Statistics Report. American Society of Plastic Surgeons. Retrieved from https://www.plasticsurgery.org/documents/News/Statistics/2016/cosmetic-procedures-ages-13-19-2016.pdf

[68] Mayer, D. T. (n.d.). Social Media's Influence on Plastic Surgery. Retrieved from The Beverly Hills Institue of Aesthetic & Reconstructive Surgery: https://bevhills.com/social-medias-influence-on-plastic-surgery/

[69] Christianity in the United States. (n.d.). Retrieved from Wikipedia: https://en.wikipedia.org/wiki/Christianity_in_the_United_States

[70] Kelly Page Anders. (2017, October 28). Retrieved from Facebook: https://www.facebook.com/kelly.burchette/posts/1917516108258878

[71] Fight the New Drug. (2017, June 23). Students From 71 High Schools Targeted by Huge Porn-Sharing Group. Retrieved from Fight the New Drug: http://fightthenewdrug.org/boys-from-70-different-schools-create-massive-porn-sharing-group-using-nudes-of-girls-at-school/

[72] Dictionary: Modesty. (n.d.). Retrieved from Google search: https://www.google.com/search?q=modesty+definition&ie=utf-8&oe=utf-8

[73] Cavazos, M. (2017, August 14). Testosterone Levels in Teenagers. Retrieved from Livestrong.com: https://www.livestrong.com/article/236521-testosterone-levels-in-teenagers/

[74] Oprah Winfrey Quotes. (n.d.). Retrieved from Brainy Quote:

https://www.brainyquote.com/quotes/quotes/o/oprahwinfr757283.html

[75] Self-Worth definition. (n.d.). Retrieved from Dictionary.com:
http://www.dictionary.com/browse/self-worth?s=t

[76] Steiner-Adair, C. (2013). The Big Disconnect. Harper-Collins

[77] Snap Inc. Terms of Service: Rights You Grant Us. (n.d.). Retrieved from Snap
Inc.: https://www.snap.com/en-US/terms/

[78] Contrera, J. (2015, May 25). A reminder that your Instagram photos aren't
really yours: Someone else can sell them for $90,000. Retrieved from
Washington Post: https://www.washingtonpost.com/news/arts-and-
entertainment/wp/2015/05/25/a-reminder-that-your-instagram-photos-arent-
really-yours-someone-else-can-sell-them-for-
90000/?utm_term=.18adcd157d53

[79] Hachman, M. (2015, October 1). The Price of Free: how Apple, Facebook,
Microsoft, and Google sell you to advertisers. Retrieved from PC World:
http://www.pcworld.com/article/2986988/privacy/the-price-of-free-how-
apple-facebook-microsoft-and-google-sell-you-to-advertisers.html

[80] Twenge, J. M. (2017, September). Have Smartphones Destroyed a
Generation? Retrieved from The Atlantic:
https://www.theatlantic.com/magazine/archive/2017/09/has-the-smartphone-
destroyed-a-generation/534198/

[81] Royal Society for Public Health. (2017, May 19). Retrieved from Instagram
ranked worst for young people's mental health:
https://www.rsph.org.uk/about-us/news/instagram-ranked-worst-for-young-
people-s-mental-health.html

[82] Sales, N. J. (2016). American Girls: Social Media and the Secret Lives of
Teenagirls. New York: Alfred A Knopf.

[83] Jean Twenge, P. (2017). iGen: Why Today's Super-Connected Kids Are
Growing Up Less Rebellious, More Tolerant, Less Happy--and Completely
Unprepared for Adulthood--and What That Means for the Rest of Us. New
York: Atria Books.

[84] Jean Twenge, P. (2017). iGen: Why Today's Super-Connected Kids Are
Growing Up Less Rebellious, More Tolerant, Less Happy--and Completely
Unprepared for Adulthood--and What That Means for the Rest of Us. New
York: Atria Books

[85] Jean Twenge, P. (2017). iGen: Why Today's Super-Connected Kids Are Growing Up Less Rebellious, More Tolerant, Less Happy--and Completely Unprepared for Adulthood--and What That Means for the Rest of Us. New York: Atria Books

[86] Jean Twenge, P. (2017). iGen: Why Today's Super-Connected Kids Are Growing Up Less Rebellious, More Tolerant, Less Happy--and Completely Unprepared for Adulthood--and What That Means for the Rest of Us. New York: Atria Books

[87] Twenge, J.M., Joiner, T.E., & Rogers, M.L. (2017). Increases in Depressive Symptoms, Suicide-Related Outcomes, and Suicide Rates Among U.S. Adolescents After 2010 and Links to Increased New Media Screen Time. *Clinical Psychological Science*, 6.

[88] Jean Twenge, P. (2017). iGen: Why Today's Super-Connected Kids Are Growing Up Less Rebellious, More Tolerant, Less Happy--and Completely Unprepared for Adulthood--and What That Means for the Rest of Us. New York: Atria Books

[89] Franklin D. Roosevelt Quotes. (n.d.). Retrieved from Good Reads: https://www.goodreads.com/author/quotes/219075.Franklin_D_Roosevelt